Microsoft Teams 2023

A Detailed Guide on Microsoft Teams With Virtual Illustrations | Learn the Tips, Tricks and Shortcuts and Become a Pro in Few Days.

BENEDICT BONNY

Copyright © 2023 BENEDICT BONNY

Do not use any part of this book in any form – electronic, mechanical or physical without an express written permission from the author.
In case of any reference to any content in this book you should make adequate reference.

Dedication

This book is dedicated to God almighty for his grace upon my life. And also, to my dad, Boniface and my late Mum, Edith Boniface for their impact in my life.

Table of Contents

Dedication iii
Acknowledgement vi
Chapter 1. 1
Introduction: Understanding Microsoft Teams and its Features 1
    The benefits of using Microsoft Teams 7
    The basic features of Microsoft Teams 9
Chapter 2 10
Setting Up Microsoft Teams 10
    Creating a Microsoft Teams account 10
    Adding team members 14
    Creating a team and channels 17
Chapter 3 26
Using Microsoft Teams for Communication 26
    Sending messages and making calls 26
    Setting up video conferences 27
    Sharing screens and files 31
Chapter 4 38
Managing Tasks and Projects with Microsoft Teams 38
    Creating tasks and assigning them to team members 38
    Using the Planner app to manage projects 42
    Integrating Microsoft Teams with other project management tools 50
Chapter 5 52
Using Microsoft Teams for Collaboration and Productivity 52
    Collaborating on documents and presentations 52
    Using the OneNote app for note-taking and sharing 53
Chapter 6 55
Security and Privacy in Microsoft Teams 55
    Protecting sensitive data and files 55
    Ensuring privacy and compliance with regulations 56
Chapter 7 59

Customizing Microsoft Teams for Your Organization 59
    Customizing themes and branding 59
    Uploading organization logo and background image 62
    Creating custom workflows and automations 65

Chapter 8 70

Troubleshooting Common Issues in Microsoft Teams 70
    Connection Issues 71
    Audio and video issues 73
    Chat and File Sharing Issues 75
    Teams meeting issues 78
    Meeting audio or video issues 79
    Meeting scheduling issues 80
    User management Issues 82
    Contacting Microsoft Teams support 84

Chapter 9 87

Advanced Tips and Tricks for Microsoft Teams 87
    Keyboard Shortcuts 87
    Time-saving Features 88
    Customizing notifications and alerts 88
    Creating custom bots and automations 90
    CONCLUSION 93
    Tips for ongoing success with Microsoft Teams 93

Acknowledgement

I would like to express my special thanks of gratitude to God Almighty who gave me the strength and wisdom to write this book.

My special thanks go to Rotimi and John who kept late nights to ensure that this book was a success.

Also, I would like to express my thanks to my siblings; Stella, Kingsley, Rita for their support and encouragement.
Would it be fair if I failed to recognize the impact other members of my family and friends also played in making this book a success? Definitely not. Every of there support is what motivated me and kept me going all through to finalize this project within the time frame. Any attempt at any level can't be satisfactorily completed without the support and guidance of you guys.
Then again, I am overwhelmed in all humbleness and gratefulness to acknowledge my depth to all those who have helped me to put these ideas well above the level of simplicity and into something concrete.

Chapter 1.

Introduction: Understanding Microsoft Teams and its Features

Microsoft Teams is a popular collaboration tool that enables remote teams to communicate and collaborate in real-time. It is an excellent platform for businesses that are looking to improve their team productivity and communication. With its extensive features, it has become a go-to tool for many businesses worldwide.

Teams is a part of the Microsoft Office 365 suite of apps and services, making it accessible to anyone with an Office 365 subscription.

The Teams platform was first introduced in 2016 as a chat-based collaboration tool that aimed to bring all Microsoft's collaboration tools under one roof. Since then, it has evolved into a robust platform with multiple features, such as video conferencing, screen sharing, file sharing, and many more.

In this guide, we will delve into some of the essential features of Microsoft Teams and how they can benefit your team.

Welcome to Teams!
Here are some things to get going...

Start chatting
Send instant messages, share files, and more over chat.
[New chat]

Meet now
Skip the calendar and create an instant meeting with just a click.
[Meet now]

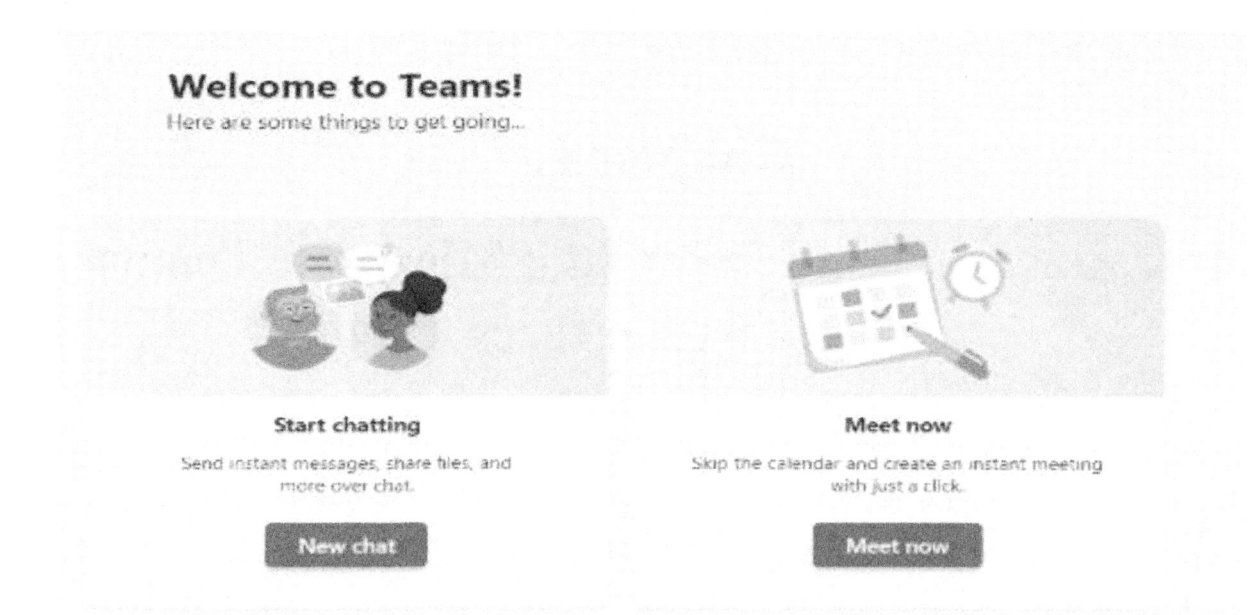

Teams and Channels

One of the most significant advantages of Microsoft Teams is the ability to create teams and channels. Teams allow businesses to group people together based on their department, function, or project. Within each team, there can be multiple channels that allow teams to organize their conversations by topics, projects, or events.

Channels are essentially chat rooms where team members can communicate, share files, and collaborate in real-time. This makes it easier for teams to communicate and collaborate without having to switch between multiple platforms.

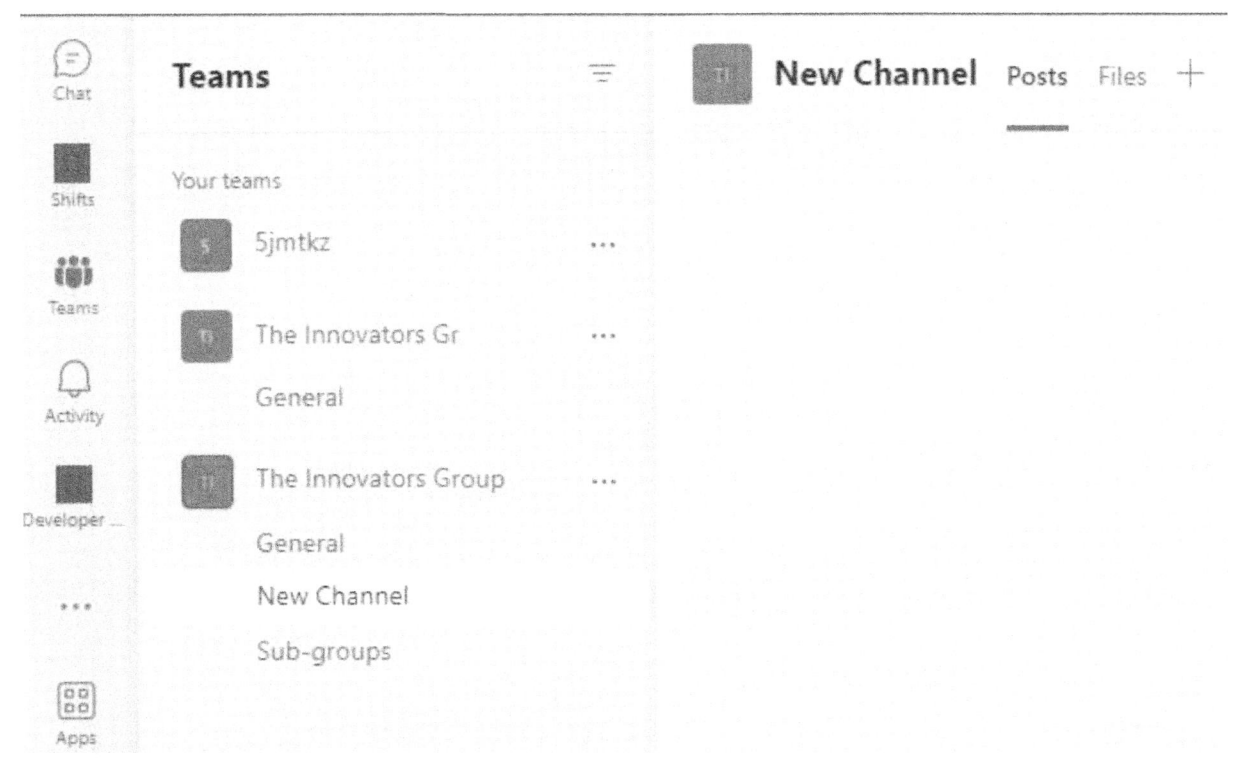

For instance, if your team is working on a specific project, you can create a channel dedicated to that project. All the team members working on the project can join the channel and communicate with each other in real-time. This ensures that everyone is on the same page and that there is no confusion about the project's progress.

Chatting and Calling

Microsoft Teams offers a range of communication tools, including chat and video conferencing. Teams have a chat feature that enables team members to communicate in real-time. This is useful when team members need to ask quick questions or when they need to share information quickly. Teams also have a calling feature that allows team members to make voice and video calls directly from the platform. This feature is particularly useful for remote teams who need to communicate frequently. It saves time and ensures that everyone is up to date with the latest developments in the project.

You're starting a new conversation

Type your first message below.

File Sharing

File sharing is a critical aspect of collaboration, and Microsoft Teams makes it easy for team members to share files with each other. Teams allow users to upload and share files directly from the platform. This means that team members can access files quickly and easily, without having to switch between multiple platforms.

Microsoft Teams also integrates with other Office 365 applications, such as OneDrive and SharePoint. This makes it easy for teams to access files that are stored in those applications.

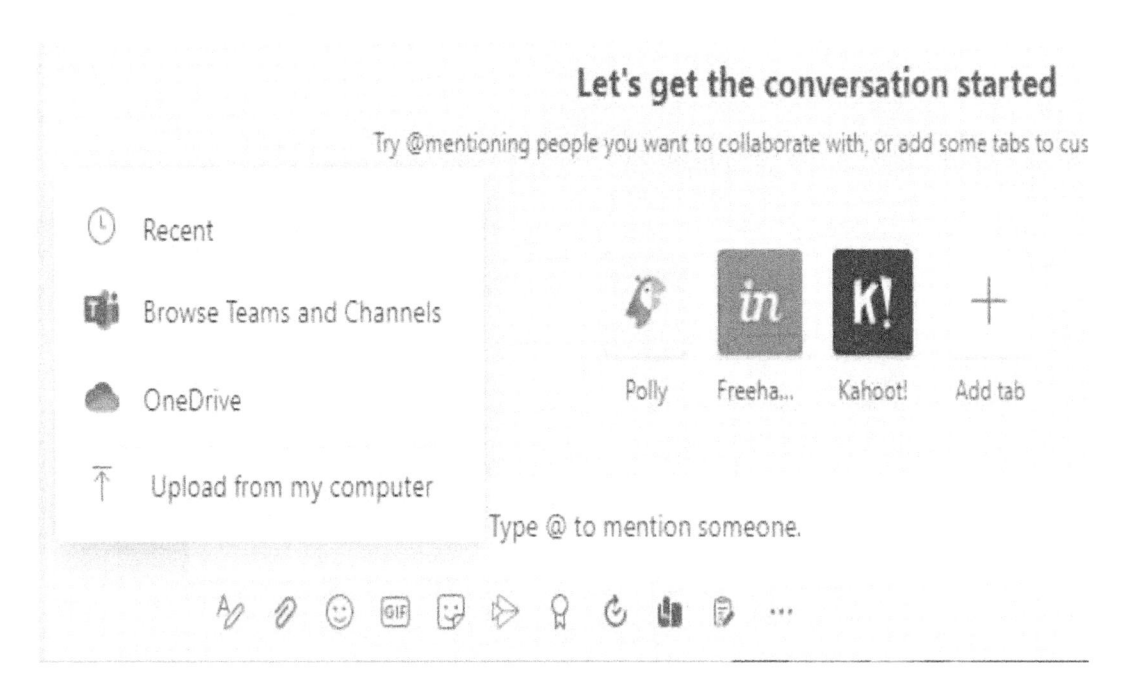

Meeting and Collaboration

Microsoft Teams has a built-in meeting and collaboration feature that enables team members to work together in real-time. The platform allows users to schedule meetings and invites team members to join the meeting.

During the meeting, team members can collaborate on files, share their screens, and make real-time edits.

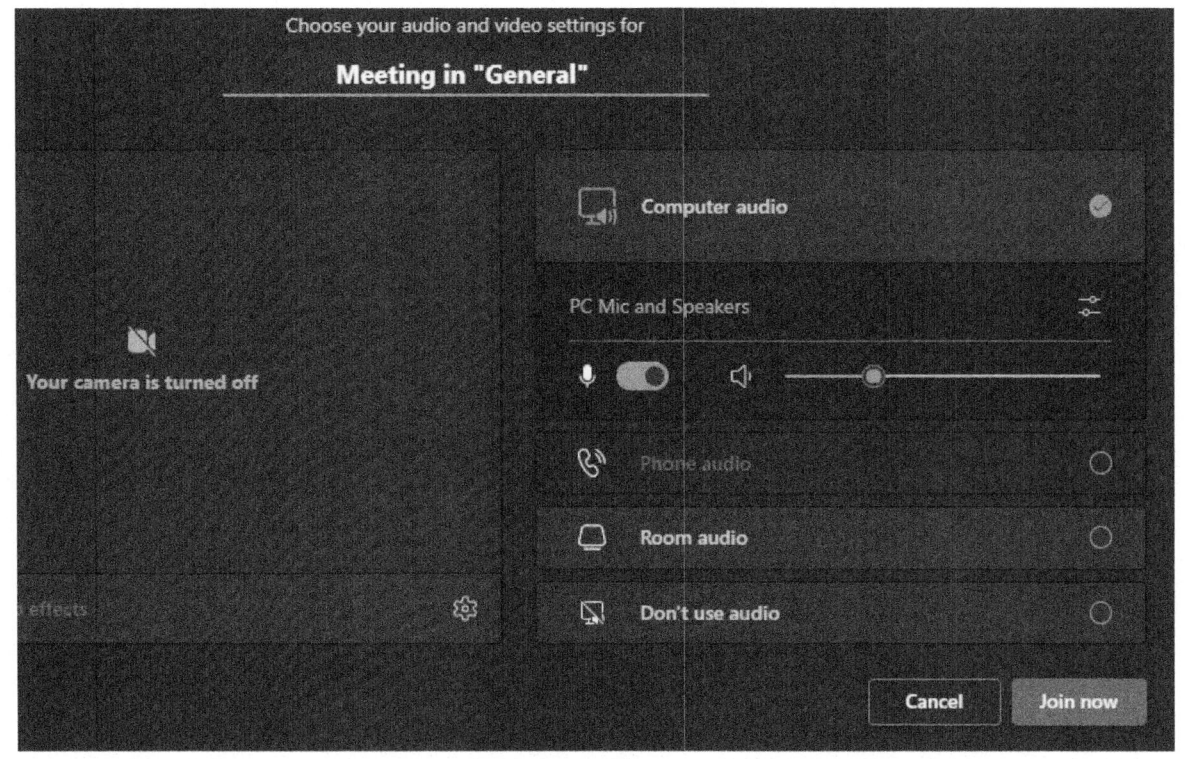

Integrations

Microsoft Teams integrates with a range of third-party apps and services. This means that teams can access their favorite apps and services directly from the Teams platform.

For instance, teams can integrate Trello, Asana, and other project management tools to the platform, enabling them to track tasks, deadlines, and progress directly from Teams. This integration makes it easier for teams to collaborate without having to switch between multiple applications.

Teams also integrates with other Microsoft apps, such as Outlook, PowerPoint, and Word. This integration allows users to access these apps directly from Teams, making it easier to collaborate on files and projects.

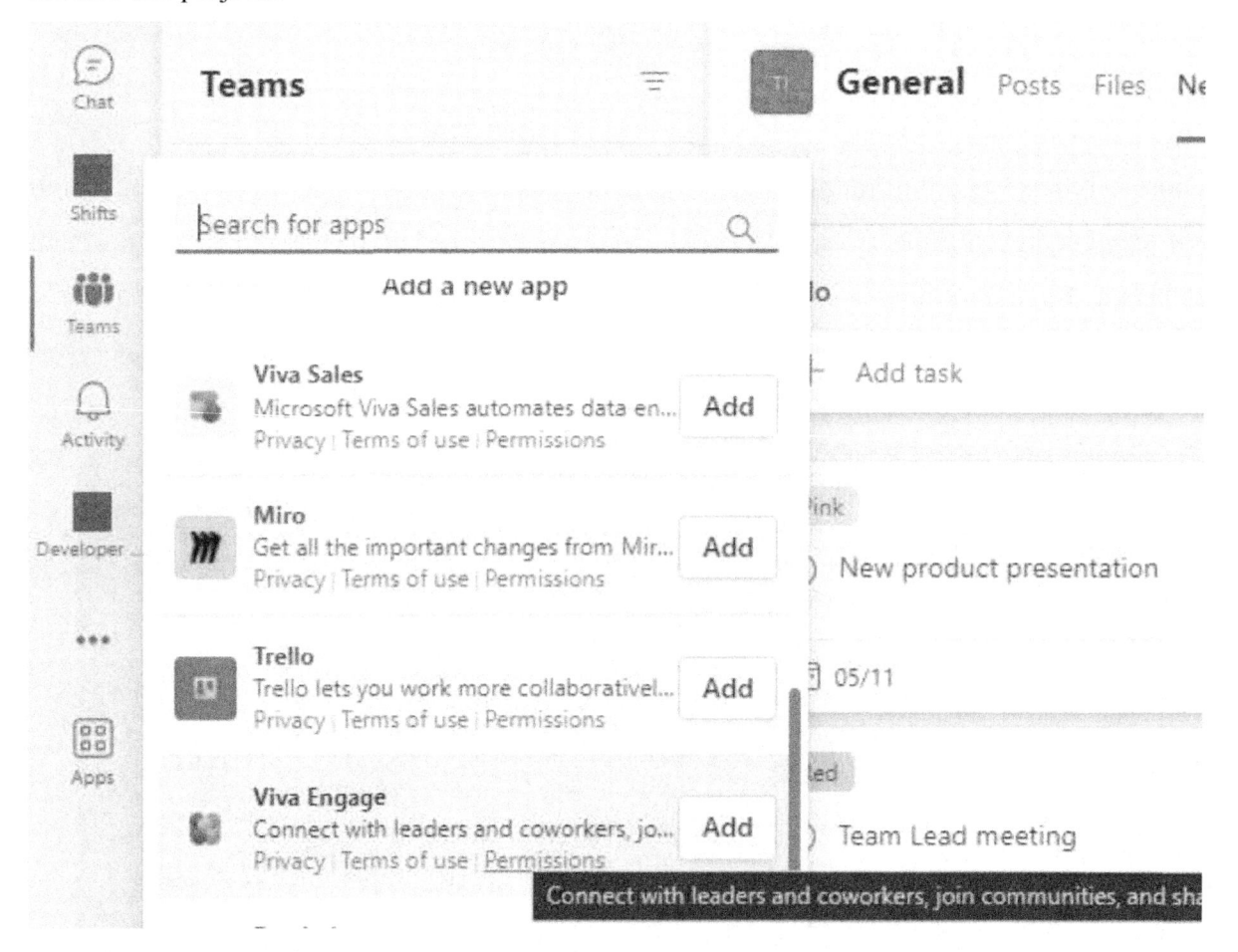

Security and Compliance

Security and compliance are critical aspects of any collaboration platform, and Microsoft Teams takes this seriously. The platform uses advanced security measures to ensure that data is protected and secure.

Teams also offers compliance features that help businesses meet regulatory and legal requirements. This ensures that businesses can use Teams without worrying about data breaches or regulatory issues.

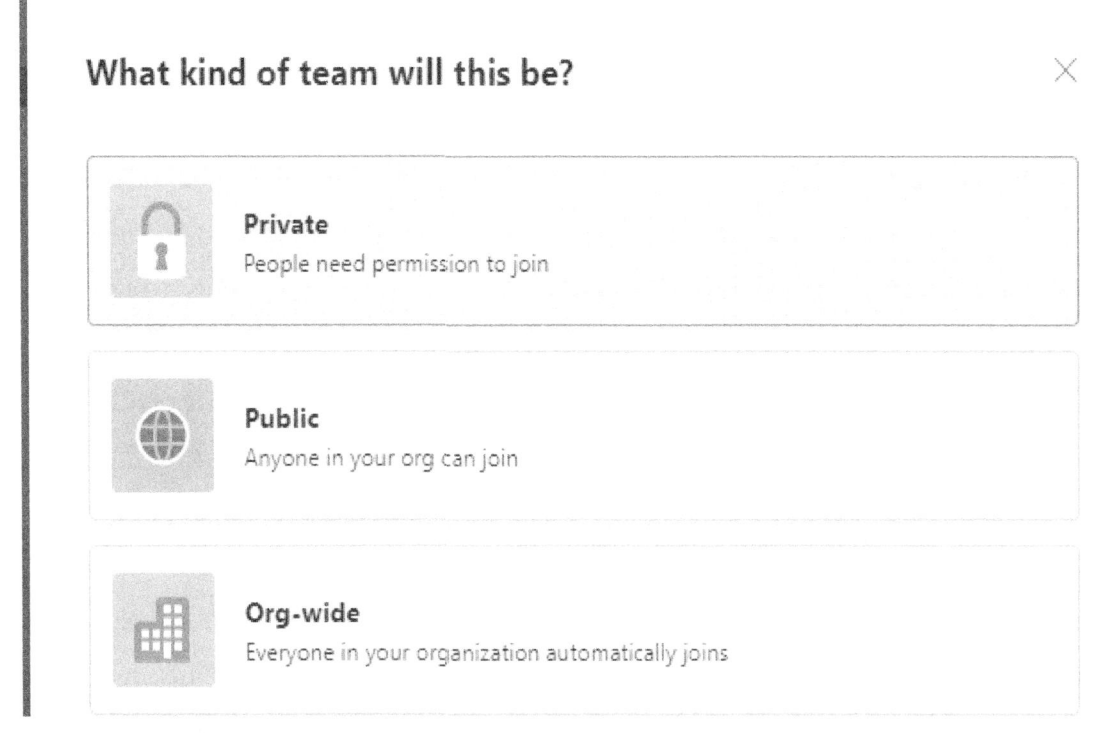

What kind of team will this be?

Private
People need permission to join

Public
Anyone in your org can join

Org-wide
Everyone in your organization automatically joins

Microsoft Teams is a powerful collaboration tool that provides a range of features that enable teams to communicate and collaborate in real-time. The platform's user-friendly interface, integration capabilities, and security features make it an excellent choice for businesses looking to improve team productivity and communication.

Teams' features, including channels, chat and calling, file sharing, meeting and collaboration, integrations, and security and compliance, make it a comprehensive and effective collaboration tool. As remote work continues to become more prevalent, Microsoft Teams is an excellent solution for businesses looking to streamline their team communication and collaboration.

The benefits of using Microsoft Teams

Microsoft Teams is fast becoming a go-to tool for businesses looking to improve team productivity and communication. Below, we will delve into the benefits of using Microsoft Teams:

Increased Productivity

Microsoft Teams is an excellent tool for businesses looking to increase team productivity. Teams' features, including chat, file sharing, and collaboration, allow team members to work together efficiently. Teams' user-friendly interface makes it easy for teams to onboard quickly and collaborate effectively.

Teams also integrates with other Microsoft apps, such as Outlook, PowerPoint, and Word, enabling teams to access these apps directly from Teams. This integration makes it easier for teams to collaborate on files and projects without having to switch between multiple applications.

Better Collaboration

Microsoft Teams' collaboration capabilities make it easier for teams to work together effectively. Teams allows businesses to create teams and channels, making it easier for teams to organize their conversations and collaborate on projects. Channels are essentially chat rooms where team members can communicate, share files, and collaborate in real-time.

Teams' file sharing capabilities make it easy for team members to share files with each other, without having to switch between multiple applications. This integration makes it easier for teams to access the files they need, leading to better collaboration and increased productivity.

Flexibility

Microsoft Teams' flexibility is another benefit that makes it an excellent collaboration tool. Teams is a cloud-based platform, which means that it can be accessed from anywhere, at any time. This makes it an ideal tool for remote teams who need to work together from different locations.

Teams also integrates with a range of third-party apps and services, enabling teams to access their favorite apps directly from Teams. This integration makes it easier for teams to collaborate without having to switch between multiple applications.

Security

Security is a critical aspect of any collaboration tool, and Microsoft Teams takes this seriously. Teams' advanced security measures ensure that data is protected and secure. Teams also offers compliance features that help businesses meet regulatory and legal requirements. This ensures that businesses can use Teams without worrying about data breaches or regulatory issues.

Cost-Effective

Microsoft Teams is a cost-effective collaboration tool, especially for businesses that already have an Office 365 subscription. Teams is included in the Office 365 suite of apps and services, which means that businesses do not need to pay extra for the platform. This makes Teams an affordable collaboration tool for businesses of all sizes.

The basic features of Microsoft Teams

Microsoft Teams allows users to communicate and work together in real-time. Here are some of its basic features:

- **Chat and messaging**: Teams allow users to send direct messages or group chats with other team members. Users can also share files and attachments within the chat.
- **Video conferencing**: Teams includes a video conferencing feature that allows users to hold meetings and collaborate with team members in real-time. It supports video and audio calls, screen sharing, and recording.
- **Team channels**: Users can create separate channels within a team to organize discussions and collaborate on specific topics or projects. Channels can be public or private and can include group chats, files, and tasks.
- **File sharing and collaboration**: Teams allows users to share files and collaborate on them in real-time. Users can work on documents together and track changes and comments.
- **Integrations**: Teams integrates with other Microsoft Office 365 applications such as OneDrive, SharePoint, and Planner, as well as third-party apps like Trello and Zoom.
- **Customization**: Teams allows users to customize their workspace by adding tabs, bots, and connectors. Bots can automate certain tasks and connectors can integrate external apps and services.
- **Mobile access**: Teams is available on desktop and mobile platforms, allowing users to access and collaborate with their team from anywhere.

Chapter 2

Setting Up Microsoft Teams

Setting up Teams can be a straightforward process, but it's important to have a clear understanding of the platform's basic features and functionalities to make the most of it. In this Chapter, we will provide an overview of the key steps involved in setting up Teams, including creating a team, adding members and setting up channels. Whether you're new to Teams or looking to optimize your existing setup, this guide will provide you with the essential information you need to get started. So, let's dive in and learn how to set up Microsoft Teams!

Creating a Microsoft Teams account

With Microsoft Teams, you can chat, hold video conferences, and share files with colleagues and classmates, regardless of where they are located. To get started with Microsoft Teams, you need to create an account. Here is how:

Step 1: Go to the Microsoft Teams website

The first step to creating a Microsoft Teams account is to visit the Microsoft Teams website. You can do this by typing "Microsoft Teams" into your web browser's search bar or by navigating directly to the website at www.microsoft.com/en-us/microsoft-teams/

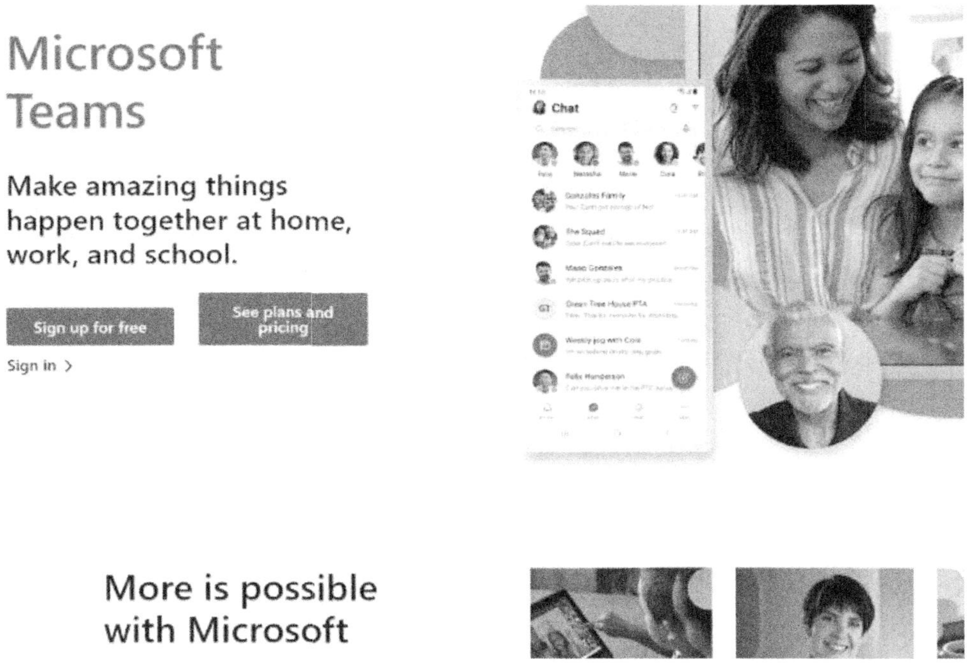

Step 2: Click "Sign up for free"

Once you are on the Microsoft Teams website, click on the "Sign up for free" button located in the middle of the page. This will take you to the sign-up page.

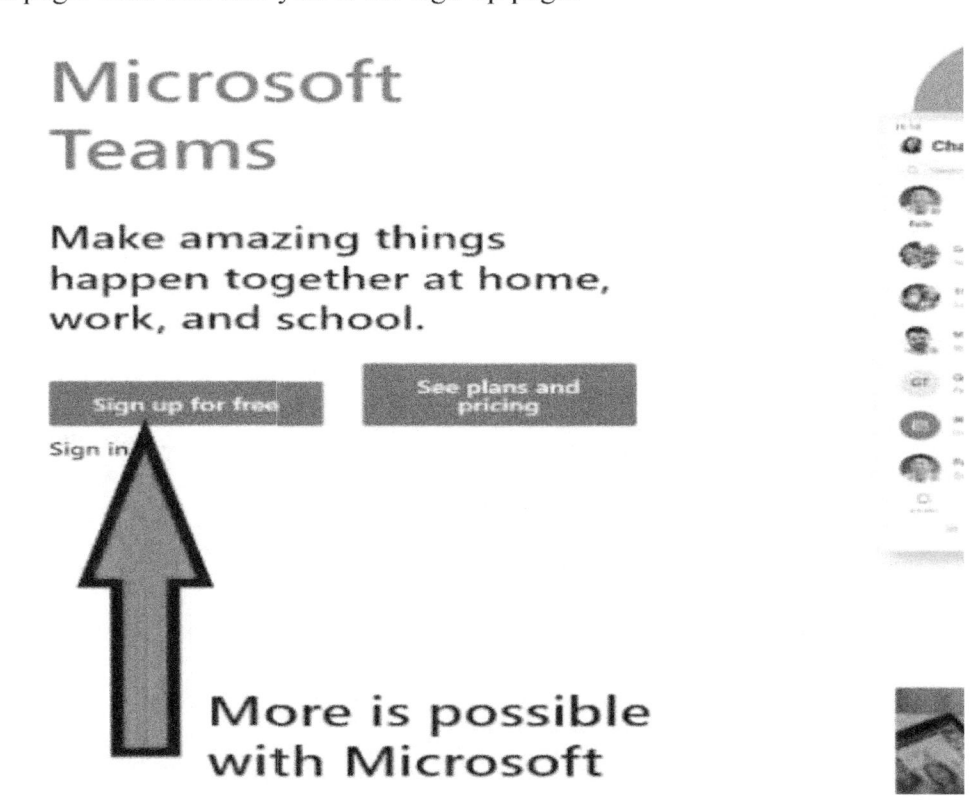

Step 3: Enter your email address

On the sign-up page, you will be prompted to enter your email address. You can use any email address you like, but it is recommended that you use your work or school email address if you plan to use Microsoft Teams for work or school purposes. If you do not have a work or school email address, you can use any other email address you have access to.

Step 4: Verify your email address

After entering your email address, Microsoft Teams will ask you to verify your email address. To do this, check your email inbox for an email from Microsoft Teams and follow the instructions to verify your email address.

Step 5: Create a password

Once your email address has been verified, you will be prompted to create a password. Make sure that your password is strong and contains a combination of letters, numbers, and symbols. You may also be asked to confirm your password by entering it again.

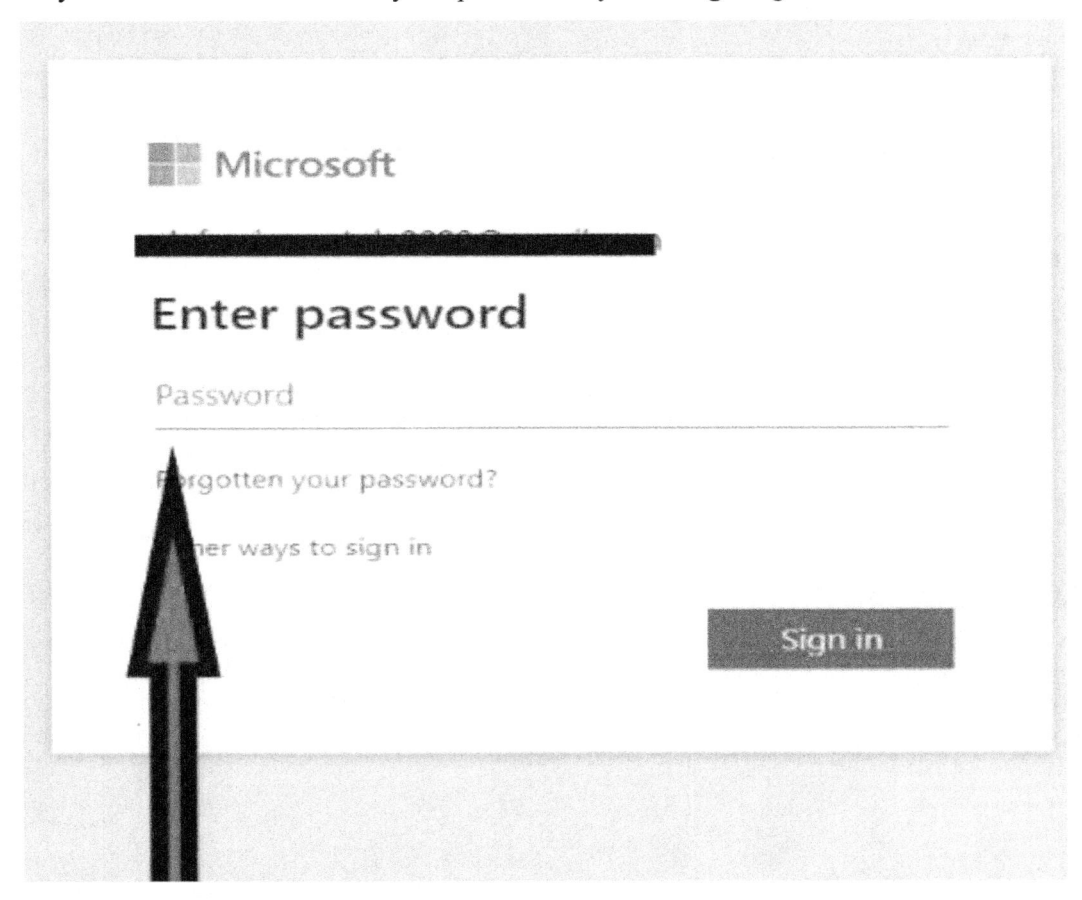

Step 6: Enter your first and last name

Next, enter your first and last name in the appropriate fields. This information will be used to identify you within Microsoft Teams.

Step 7: Click "Set up Teams"

After entering your name, click on the "Set up Teams" button. This will take you to the Teams setup page.

Step 8: Choose your organization type

On the Teams setup page, you will be asked to choose your organization type. You can choose from three options: business, education, or government. Select the option that best describes your organization.

Step 9: Enter your organization's name

Once you have chosen your organization type, you will be prompted to enter your organization's name. This is the name that will be displayed to other members of your organization in Microsoft Teams.

Step 10: Choose your role

After entering your organization's name, you will be asked to choose your role within the organization. You can choose from three options: teacher/educator, student, or other. Select the option that best describes your role within the organization.

Step 11: Click "Create"

Once you have entered all of the required information, click on the "Create" button. This will create your Microsoft Teams account.

Step 12: Download the Microsoft Teams app

After creating your account, you will be prompted to download the Microsoft Teams app. You can download the app for Windows, Mac, iOS, or Android, depending on the device you are using.

Step 13: Log in to Microsoft Teams

Once you have downloaded the Microsoft Teams app, log in using the email address and password you used to create your account. You will now be able to use Microsoft Teams to chat, hold video conferences, and share files with others in your organization.

Adding team members

Once you have created a team in Microsoft Teams, you can add team members to it, allowing them to access and contribute to the team's files, conversations, and meetings. To do this:

Step 1: Open Microsoft Teams

The first step to adding team members to your Microsoft Teams account is to open the Microsoft Teams app on your device. You can access Microsoft Teams on your computer, tablet, or mobile device.

Step 2: Select the team you want to add members

Once you have opened Microsoft Teams, select the team you want to add members to. You can do this by clicking on the "Teams" icon on the left-hand side of the app and then selecting the team from the list of teams you are a member of.

Step 3: Click on "More options"

After selecting the team, click on the "More options" icon located in the upper right-hand corner of the screen. The icon looks like three dots arranged vertically.

Step 4: Select "Add member"

From the "More options" menu, select "Add member." This will bring up a dialog box where you can add team members.

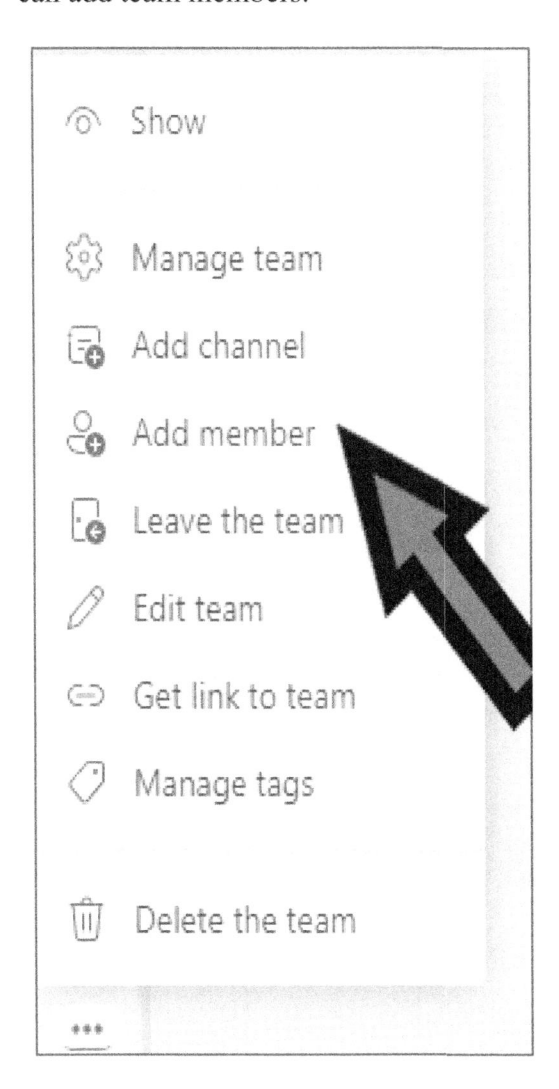

Step 5: Enter the email address of the person you want to add

In the dialog box, enter the email address of the person you want to add to the team. You can also add multiple email addresses at once by separating them with a semicolon.

Step 6: Choose the permission level for the new member

Next, choose the permission level for the new member. You can choose from three options:

Owner: Owners have full control over the team and can add or remove members, change team settings, and delete the team.

Member: Members can contribute to the team's conversations and files, but cannot make changes to the team's settings.

Guest: Guests are external users who are not part of your organization but need access to the team's files and conversations. Guests have limited access to team features and settings.

Step 7: Click "Add"

After entering the email address and choosing the permission level, click on the "Add" button. This will send an invitation to the person you want to add to the team.

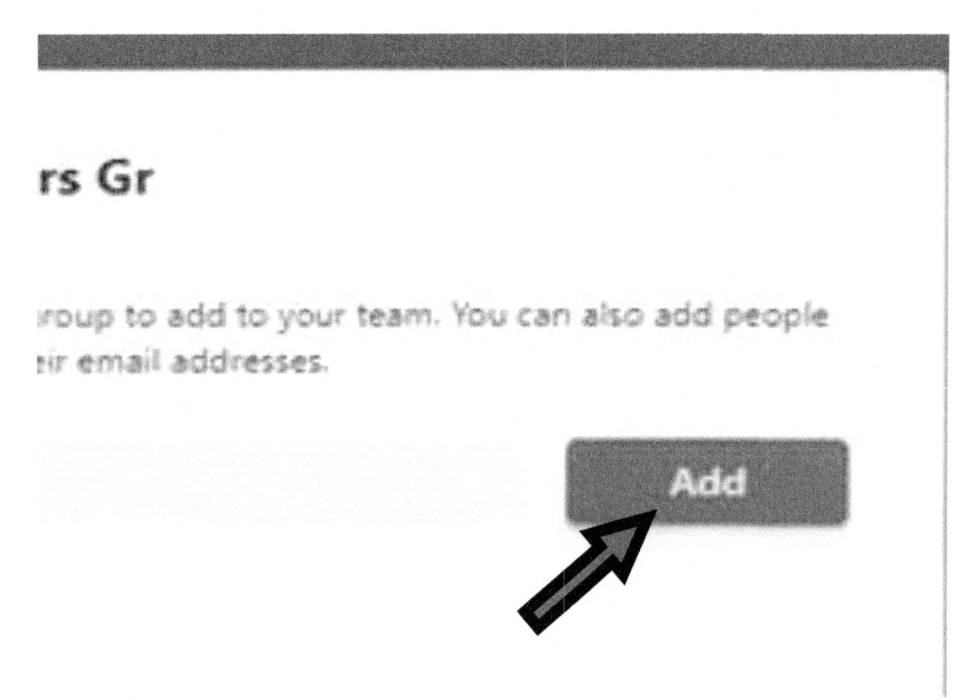

Step 8: Wait for the new member to accept the invitation

Once you have added the new member, they will receive an email invitation to join the team. They will need to click on the link in the email and sign in to Microsoft Teams using their Microsoft account or create a new account if they do not already have one. Once they have accepted the invitation, they will be added to the team.

Step 9: Manage team members

Once you have added team members, you can manage their permissions and settings by clicking on the "More options" icon in the upper right-hand corner of the screen and selecting "Manage team." From here, you can add or remove members, change their permission levels, and customize team settings.

Tips for Adding Team Members
- Make sure to enter the correct email address for the person you want to add. If you enter the wrong email address, the invitation will be sent to the wrong person, and they will not be able to join the team.
- Choose the appropriate permission level for each team member based on their role in the organization and their need for access to team features and settings.
- Be sure to communicate with team members about any changes to team settings or permissions. This can help prevent confusion and ensure that everyone is on the same page.
- Keep the team membership list up to date by removing members who are no longer part of the organization

Creating a team and channels

The first step in using Microsoft Teams is to create a team. A team is a group of people who work together on a specific project or goal. Here's how you can create a team on Microsoft Teams:

Step 1: Launch Microsoft Teams and sign in to your account.

Step 2: Click on the "Teams" tab on the left-hand side of the screen.

Step 3: Click on the "Join or create a team" button.

Step 4: Select "Create a team" from the options

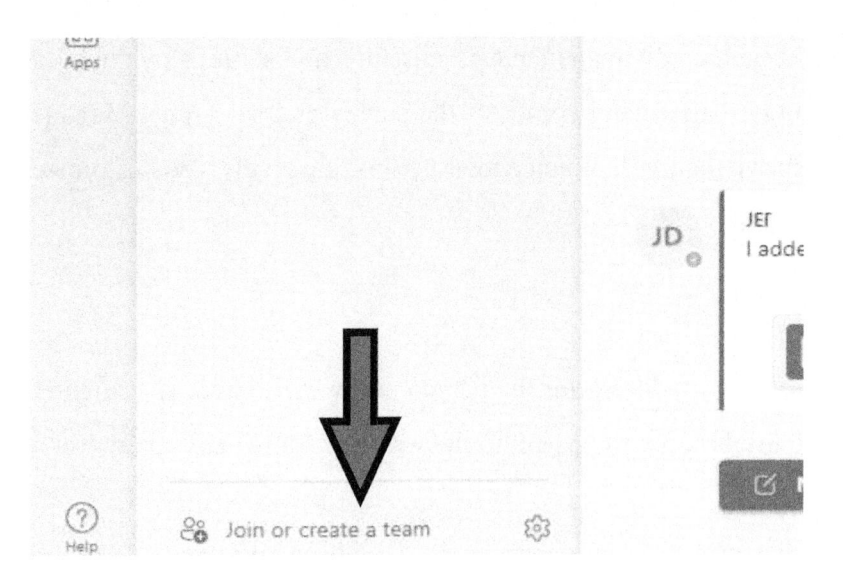

Step 5: Choose the type of team you want to create. You can select from the following options:

    a) **Standard**: This is a team that is created from scratch.

    b) **Class**: This is a team designed for teachers and students to work together.

    c) **Professional Learning Community** (**PLC**): This is a team designed for educators to collaborate and share resources.

    d) **Staff**: This is a team designed for school staff to collaborate and share resources.

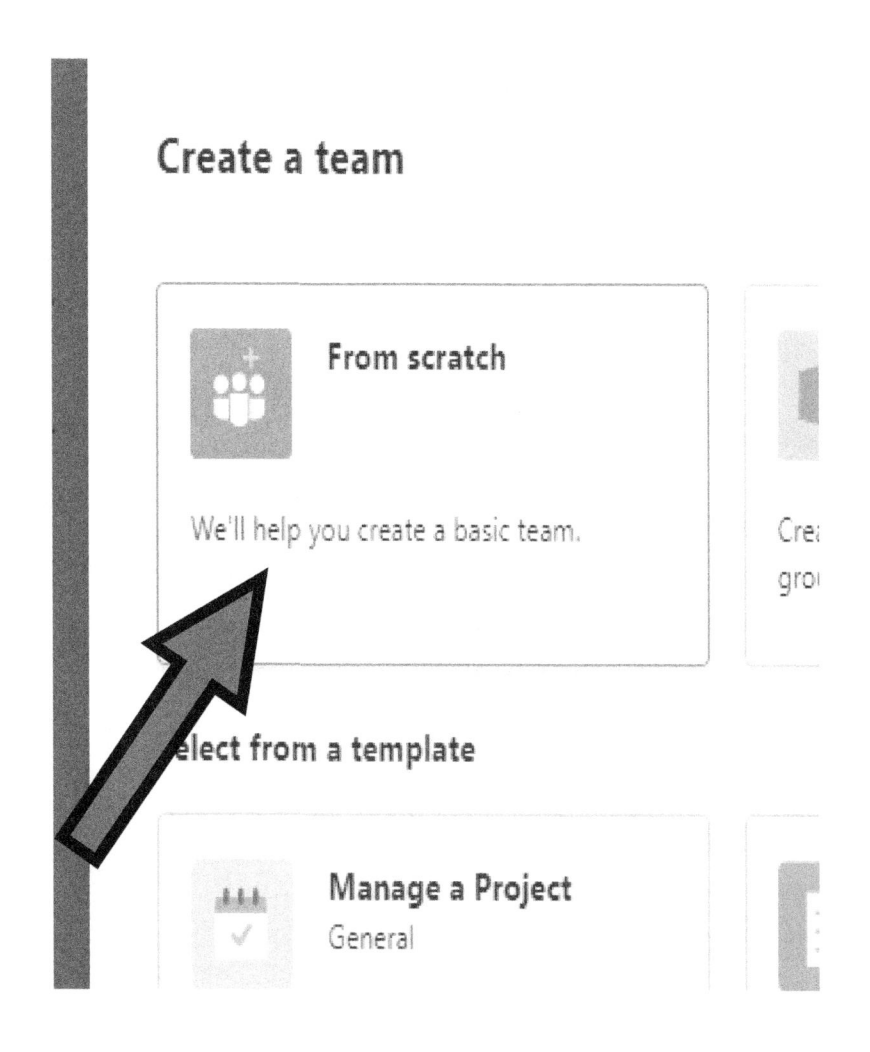

Step 6: Choose a team name and add a short description.

Step 7: Choose the privacy settings for your team. You can choose from the following options:
   a) Public: Anyone in your organization can join the team.
   b) Private: Only the members you invite can join the team.

Step 8: Click on the "Create" button to create your team.

Creating Channels

Once you have created a team, the next step is to create channels. A channel is a specific topic or area of focus within a team. It is a great way to organize your team's work and keep everyone on the same page. Here's how you can create channels on Microsoft Teams:

Step 1: Go to the team that you want to create a channel for.

Step 2: Click on the "More options" (three dots) button next to the team's name.

Step 3: Select "Add channel" from the options.

Step 4: Choose a name for your channel and add a short description.

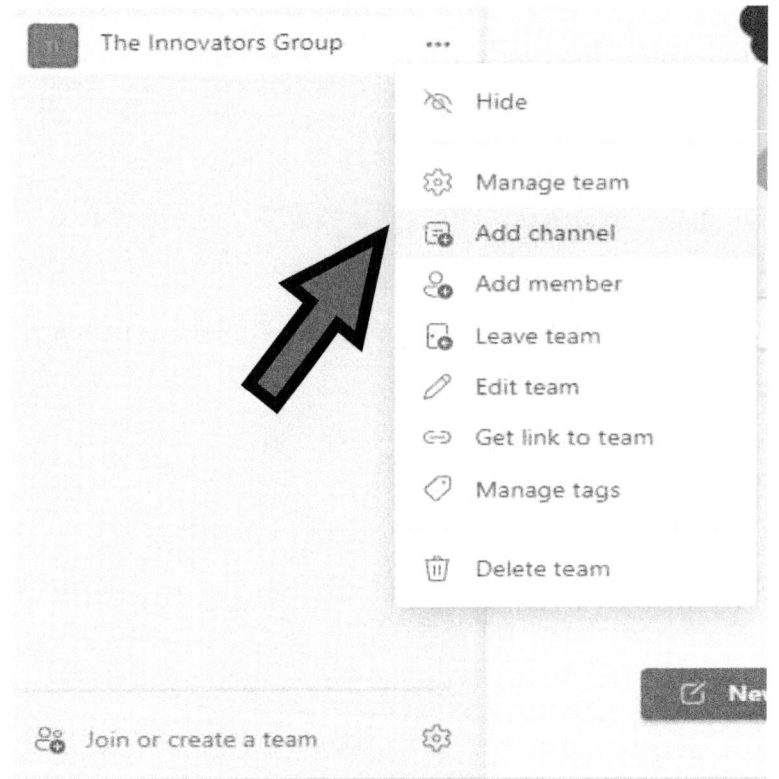

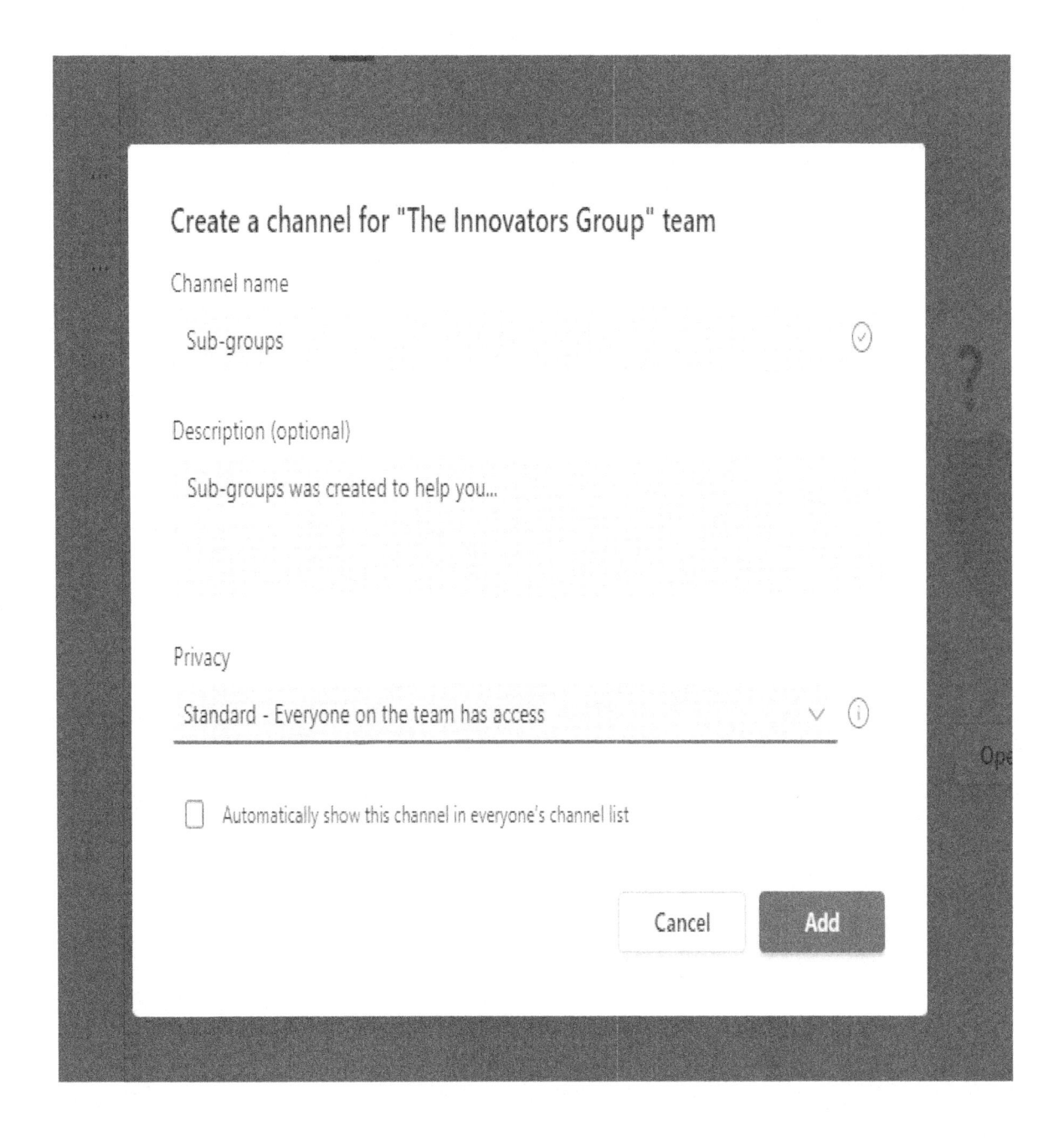

Step 5: Choose the privacy settings for your channel. You can choose from the following options:
   a) **Standard**: This is the default setting, and anyone in the team can see and participate in the channel.
   b) **Private**: Only the members you invite can see and participate in the channel.

Step 6: Click on the "Add" button to create your channel.

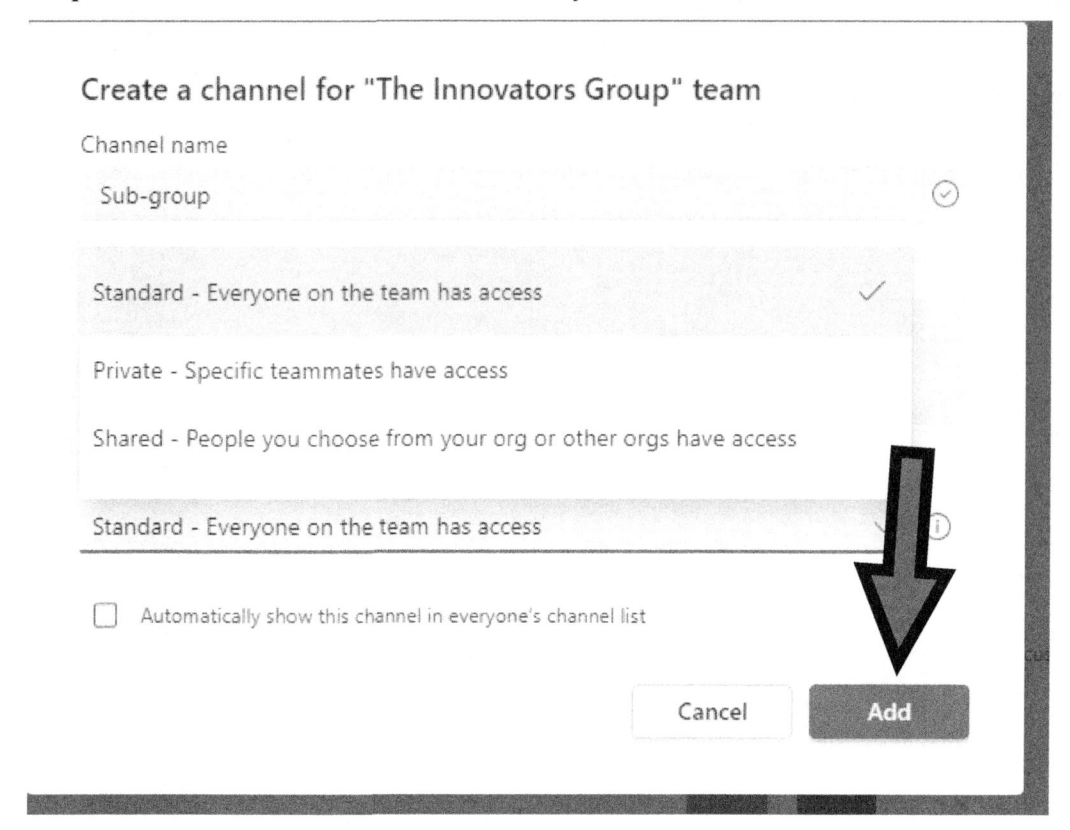

Create a channel for "The Innovators Group" team

Channel name

Sub-group

Standard - Everyone on the team has access

Private - Specific teammates have access

Shared - People you choose from your org or other orgs have access

Standard - Everyone on the team has access

☐ Automatically show this channel in everyone's channel list

Cancel   **Add**

Managing Channel

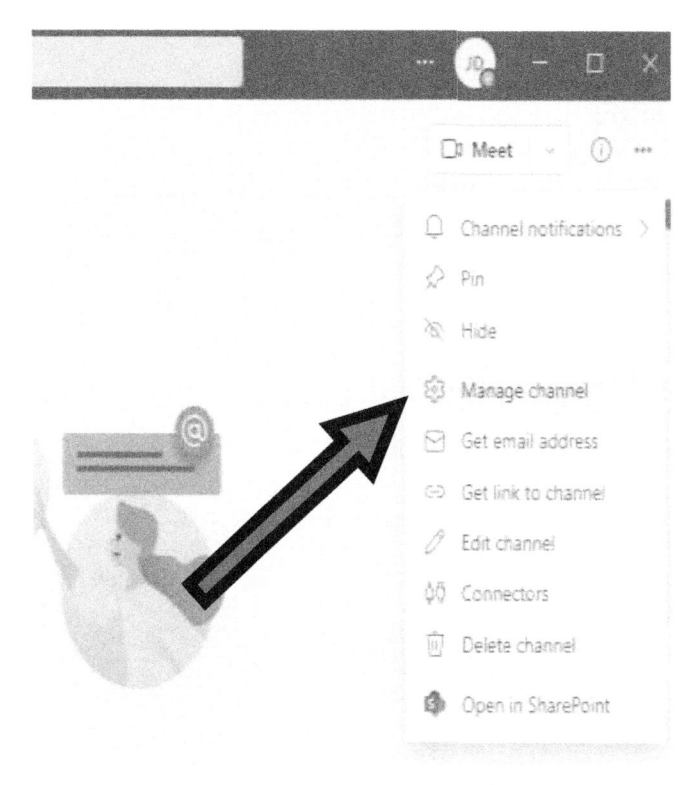

After creating channels, you may need to manage them to keep your team organized and productive. Here are some tips on how to manage your channels:

- **Pin Important Channels**: You can pin important channels to the top of the team's channel list. This makes it easy for team members to access the most critical channels.

- **Archive Unused Channels**: If a channel is no longer in use, you can archive it. Archiving a channel makes it read-only, and it can be unarchived at any time.

- **Rename Channels**: If the name of a channel no longer reflects its purpose, you can rename it. Renaming a channel doesn't affect its content or settings.

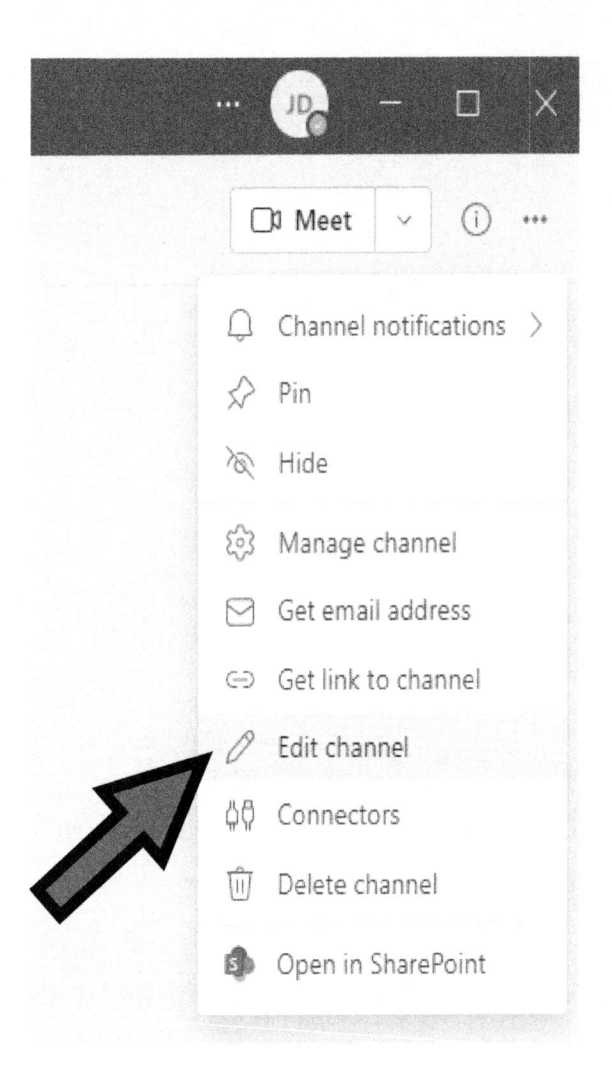

- **Delete Channels**: If a channel is no longer needed, you can delete it. Deleting a channel permanently removes its content and settings.

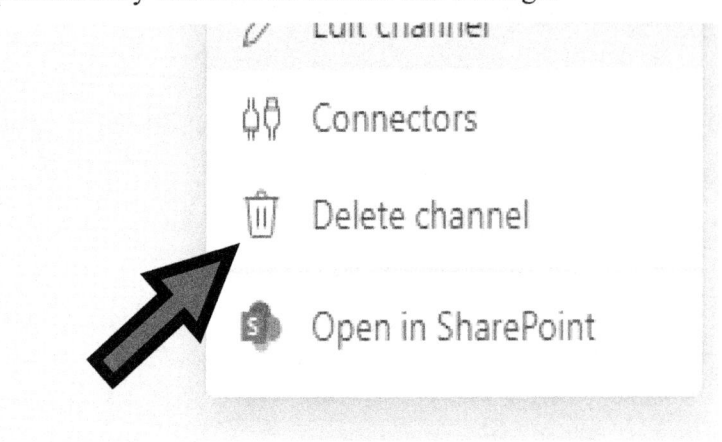

- **Change Channel Settings**: You can change the privacy settings and other channel settings at any time.

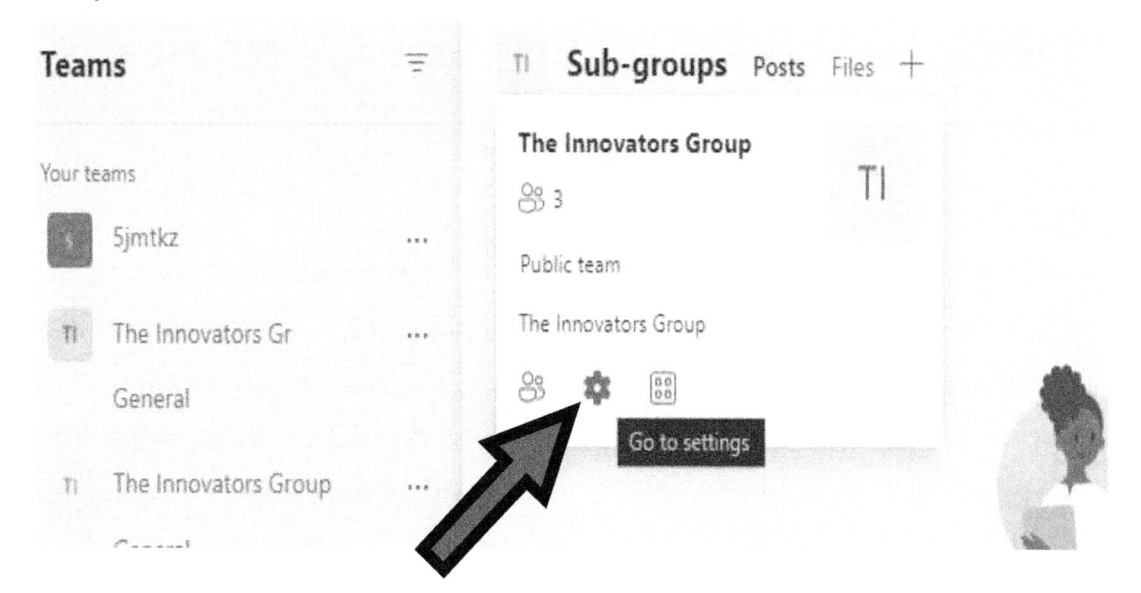

Chapter 3

Using Microsoft Teams for Communication

Sending messages and making calls

Users are able to send text messages to one or more members of their team via the instant messaging functionality of Microsoft Teams, which is one of the most important elements of this collaboration platform. On Teams, sending a message is as easy as selecting the individual or group you want to communicate with, typing your message, and clicking the send button.

On Teams, you may send a wide variety of communications, such as text messages, emoticons, and GIFs. Text messages are one of the more common sorts of messages. Users have the ability to format their messages in a number of different ways, including using bold, italic, and underlined text; bullet points; and numbers.

Users have the ability to not only send messages to specific members of a team but also to the various channels that are contained inside a team. Channels are areas within a team that are set aside specifically for particular subjects or initiatives, and they are an excellent method to maintain conversational order and concentration.

All of the users who are subscribed to a certain channel will be notified whenever that channel receives a new message. Teams will find it much simpler to maintain an up-to-date knowledge of the most recent advancements and to collaborate in real time as a result of this.

Participating in audio calls with Microsoft Teams

Microsoft Teams enables users to make voice calls in addition to allowing them to send text messages. Users are able to have talks in real time with their coworkers and team members thanks to this feature, which eliminates the requirement for a separate phone system or application.

On Teams, all you need to do to start a voice call is click the phone icon after you have chosen the person or group you wish to speak with. If the individual or organization in question is currently online, the call will be put through instantly. If the person or organization being called is not currently available, the call will be transferred to voicemail.

Users have the ability to mute or unmute their microphone, turn on or off their camera, and share their screen with other participants while they are on a voice conversation. Even if members of a team are located in different regions of the world, it is much simpler for them to cooperate and work together because to the ease that this provides.

Using Microsoft Teams for video chats and calls

Last but not least, Microsoft Teams features video calls, which enable users to have face-to-face chats with their coworkers and other members of their team. Video calls are an excellent tool for fostering the development of connections, fostering increased collaboration, and enhancing communication among members of a team.

When using Teams, all you need to do to make a video call is pick the person or group you want to talk to and then click the video icon. If the individual or organization in question is currently online, the call will be put through instantly. If the person or organization being called is not currently available, the call will be transferred to voicemail.

Users are able to see and hear other participants during a video call, as well as share their screen, engage in conversation with other users, and record the session for use at a later time. Even if members of a team are located in different regions of the world, it is much simpler for them to cooperate and work together because to the ease that this provides.

Setting up video conferences

In this section, we will investigate the numerous capabilities that are available on Microsoft Teams as well as the actions that must be taken in order to set up and hold video conferences.

Step 1: start a new meeting in Teams.

To initiate a brand-new video conference in Teams, you will initially have to go to the calendar tab that is located on the left-hand side of the Teams user interface. To begin setting up a new video conference, navigate to the previous page and click on the button labeled "New Meeting."

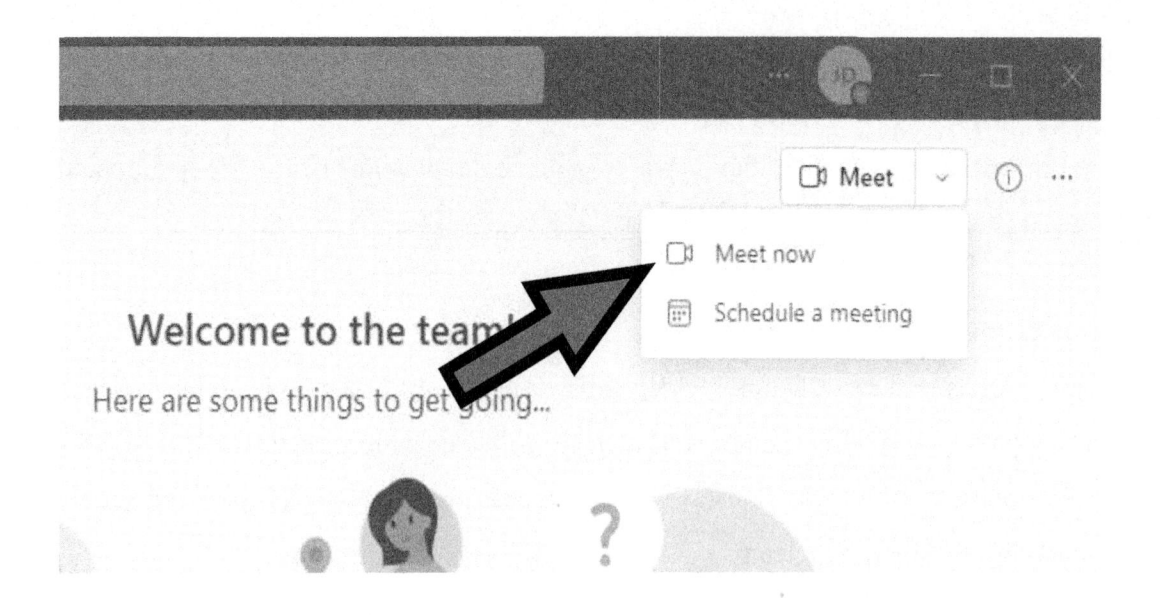

Step 2: Determining who will participate and setting a time and place for the meeting

After you have produced a new meeting, you will be required to choose the attendees that you wish to invite and then set a time for the meeting. You will be able to accomplish this by entering the attendees' email addresses into the "Attendees" column and selecting a day and time for the meeting.

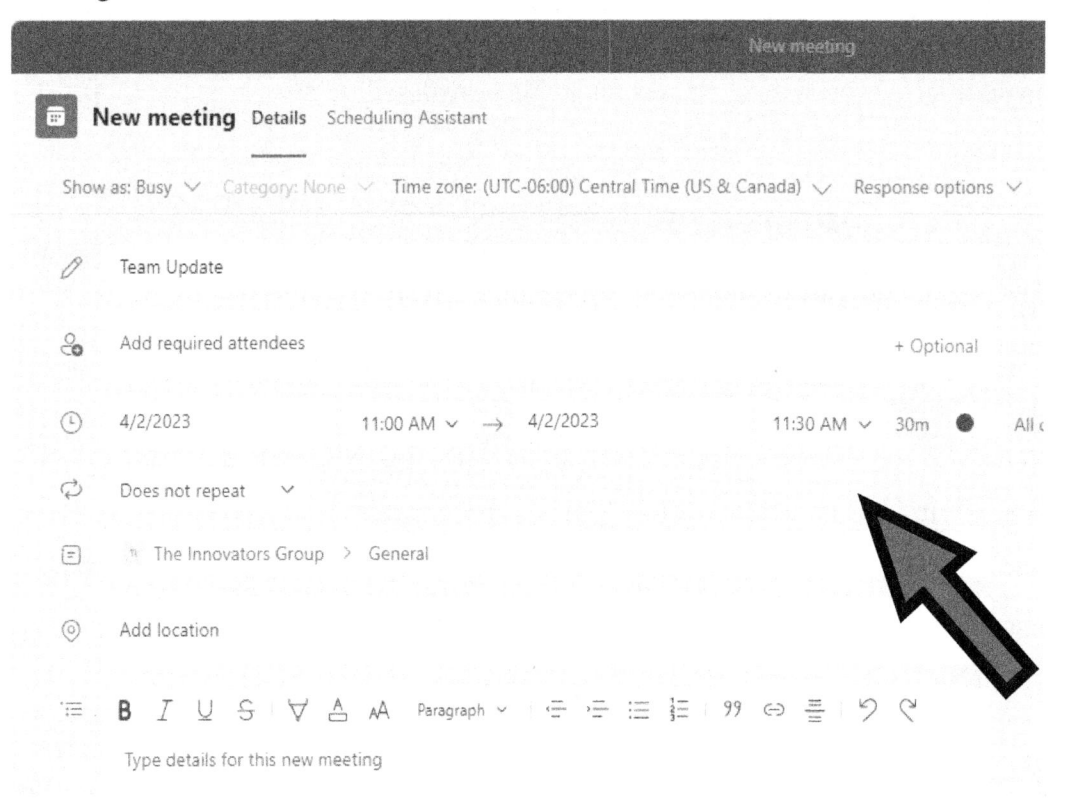

If you need to arrange video conferences on a regular basis, you may also set up a meeting that happens on a defined schedule. This can be especially helpful for meetings of a team, status reports on a project, or other forms of regular meetings.

Step 3: Make your selections for the video and audio settings.
After you have the meeting planned, you will be prompted to select the video and audio options for the event. This includes deciding the camera and microphone to use, as well as modifying the settings for your audio volume and video quality.

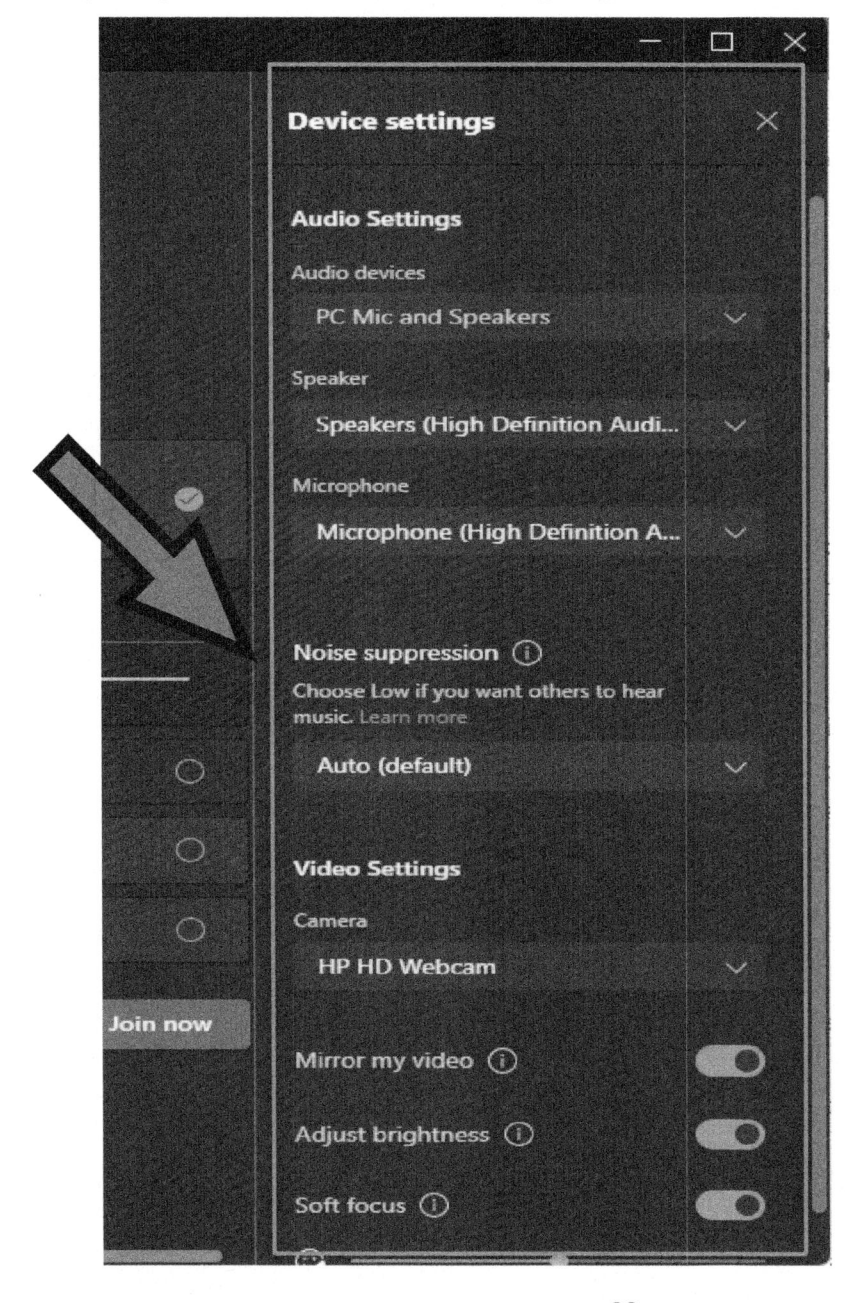

You also have the option throughout the meeting to share your screen with the other attendees, which can be helpful for activities such as demonstrations, presentations, or group work sessions. In addition, based on the tastes and requirements of individual participants, you have the option to either turn the video and audio on or off for them.

Step 4: Attend the meeting.

When it comes time for the video conference, participants can join the meeting by either clicking on the link in the email invitation they received or by navigating to the calendar tab in Teams and selecting the meeting from the list of upcoming events.

Once everyone has joined the meeting, they will be able to communicate with one another through the chat feature, as well as make use of the video and audio capabilities to converse and work together. In addition, participants can share either their screens or the files on their computers with one another, depending on the requirements of the conference.

Step 5: Taking charge of the gathering

You will have access to a variety of resources and choices as the conference manager, given that you are the host of the meeting. This includes the capability to mute or unmute participants, turn participants' videos on or off, and remove participants from the meeting if it becomes essential to do so.

You may also use the "Record" tool to record the meeting for future reference, and you can use the "Live Event" feature to host large-scale webinars or presentations with up to 10,000 attendees each time. Both of these features are accessible through the "Meetings" tab on the main navigation bar.

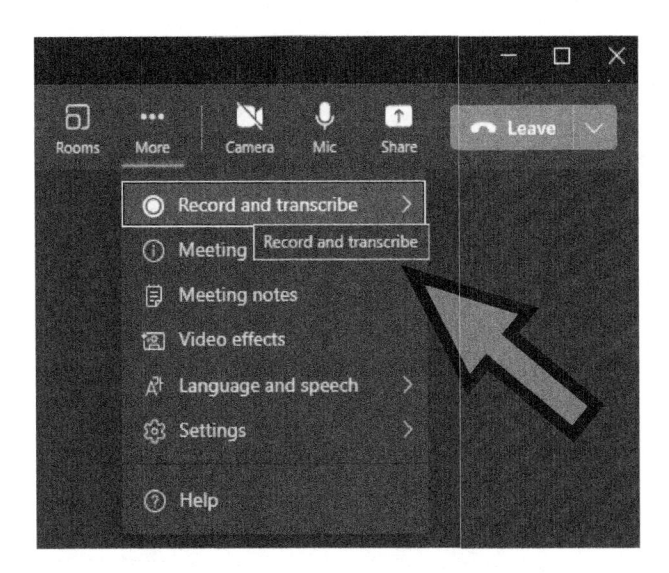

Sharing screens and files

In this section, we'll explore the steps involved in sharing screens and files on Microsoft Teams.

Sharing screens on Microsoft Teams

Sharing your screen is a useful feature when you need to collaborate with colleagues or show a presentation to a group. Here are the steps to share your screen on Microsoft Teams:

Step 1: **Start a call or meeting**

To share your screen, you first need to start a call or meeting. You can do this by clicking on the "Meet" icon on the left-hand side of the Teams interface, or by scheduling a meeting using the calendar feature.

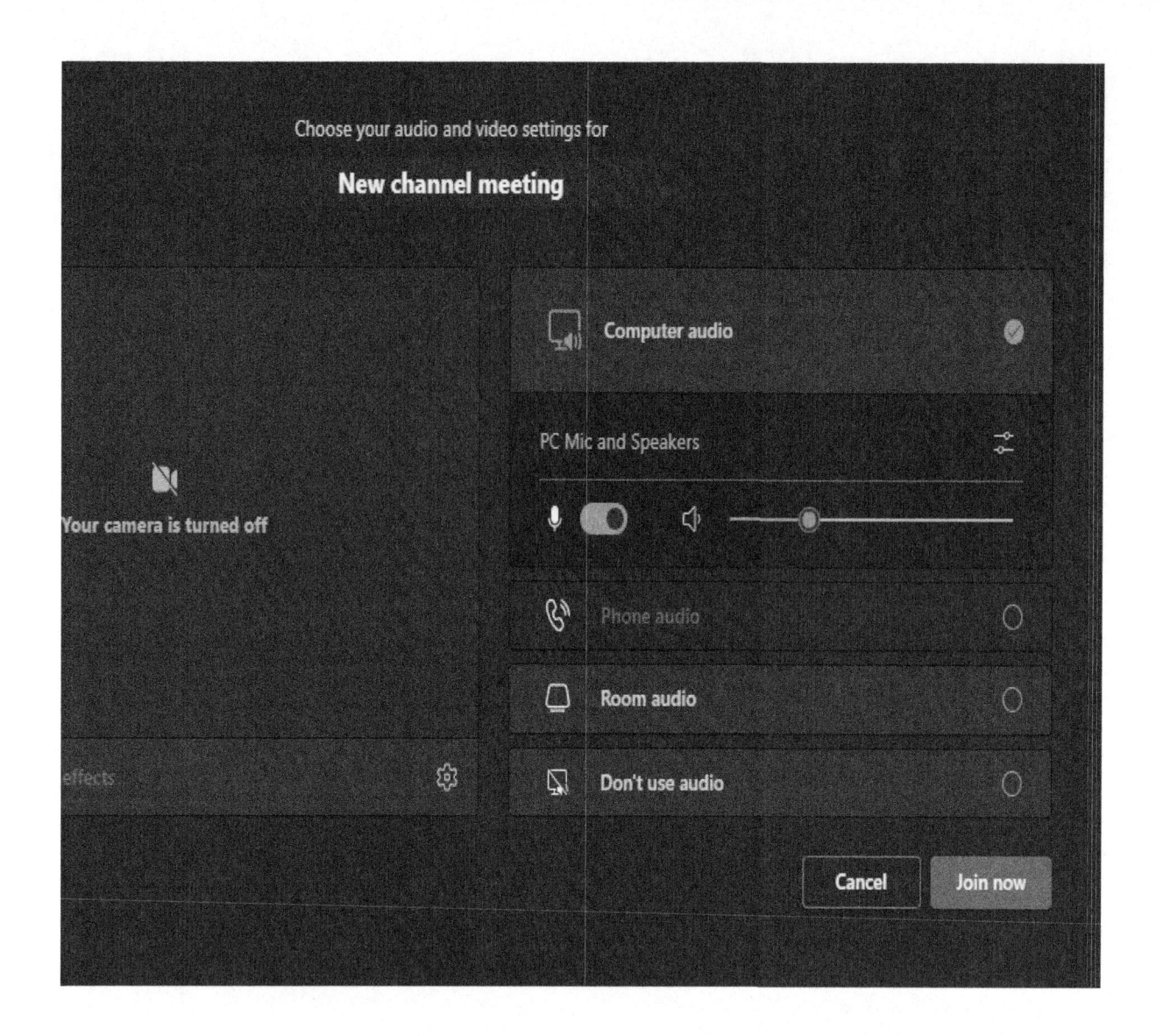

Step 2: Click on the "Share" icon

Once you are in a call or meeting, click on the "Share" icon located in the toolbar at the bottom of the screen. This will bring up a menu of options for sharing your screen.

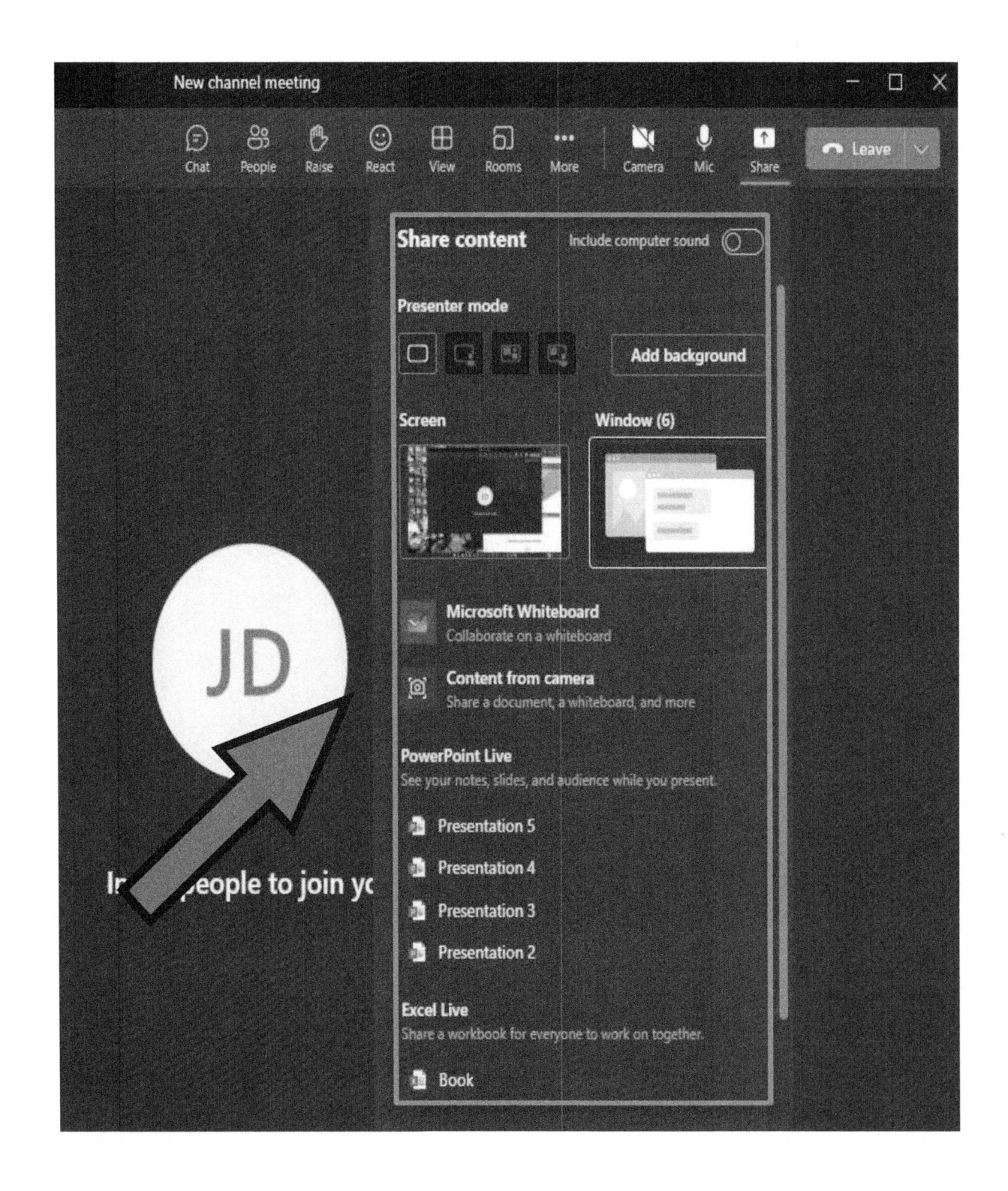

Step 3: Choose the screen to share

From the menu of options, select the screen you want to share with your colleagues. You can choose to share your entire screen, or just a specific application or window.

Step 4: Start sharing your screen

Once you've selected the screen you want to share, click the "Share" button to start sharing your screen with your colleagues. You can also choose to share audio along with your screen, which can be useful if you are presenting a video or audio clip.

Step 5: Stop sharing your screen

To stop sharing your screen, simply click the "Stop Sharing" button located in the toolbar at the bottom of the screen. This will end the screen sharing session and return you to the call or meeting.

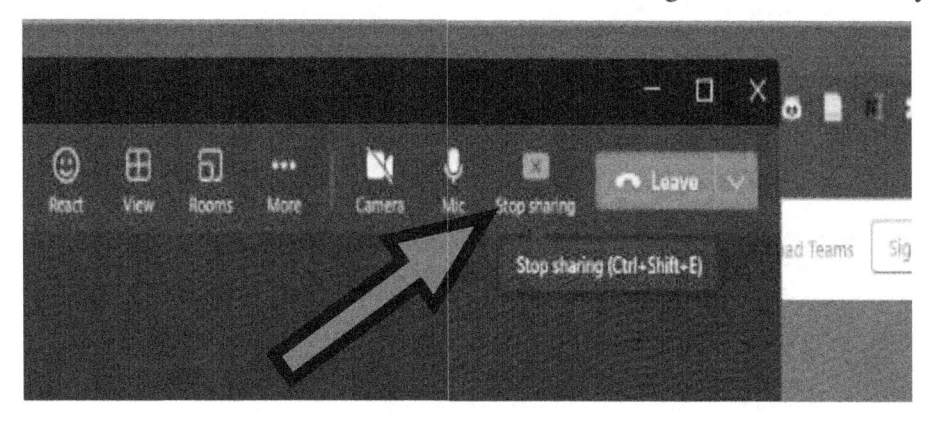

Sharing files on Microsoft Teams

Sharing files on Microsoft Teams is a convenient way to collaborate on documents, spreadsheets, and other types of files with colleagues. Here are the steps to share files on Microsoft Teams:

Step 1: Open the Teams chat

To share a file, you first need to open the chat window in Teams. You can do this by clicking on the chat icon located on the left-hand side of the Teams interface.

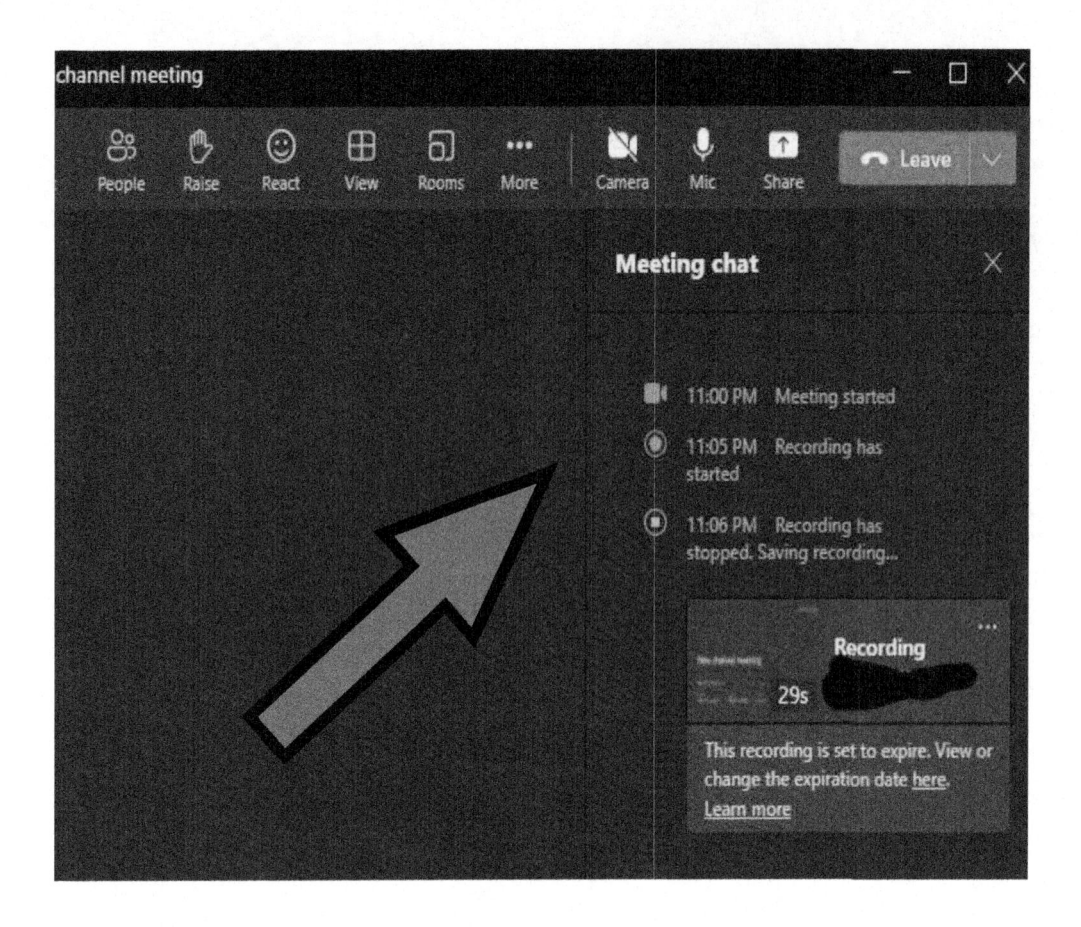

Step 2: Select the person or group you want to share the file with

From the chat window, select the person or group you want to share the file with. You can do this by typing their name in the search bar located at the top of the chat window.

Step 3: Click on the "Attach" icon

Once you've selected the person or group you want to share the file with, click on the "Attach" icon located in the toolbar at the bottom of the chat window. This will bring up a menu of options for sharing files.

Step 4: Choose the file you want to share

From the menu of options, select the file you want to share with your colleagues. You can choose to share files from your computer, OneDrive, or SharePoint.

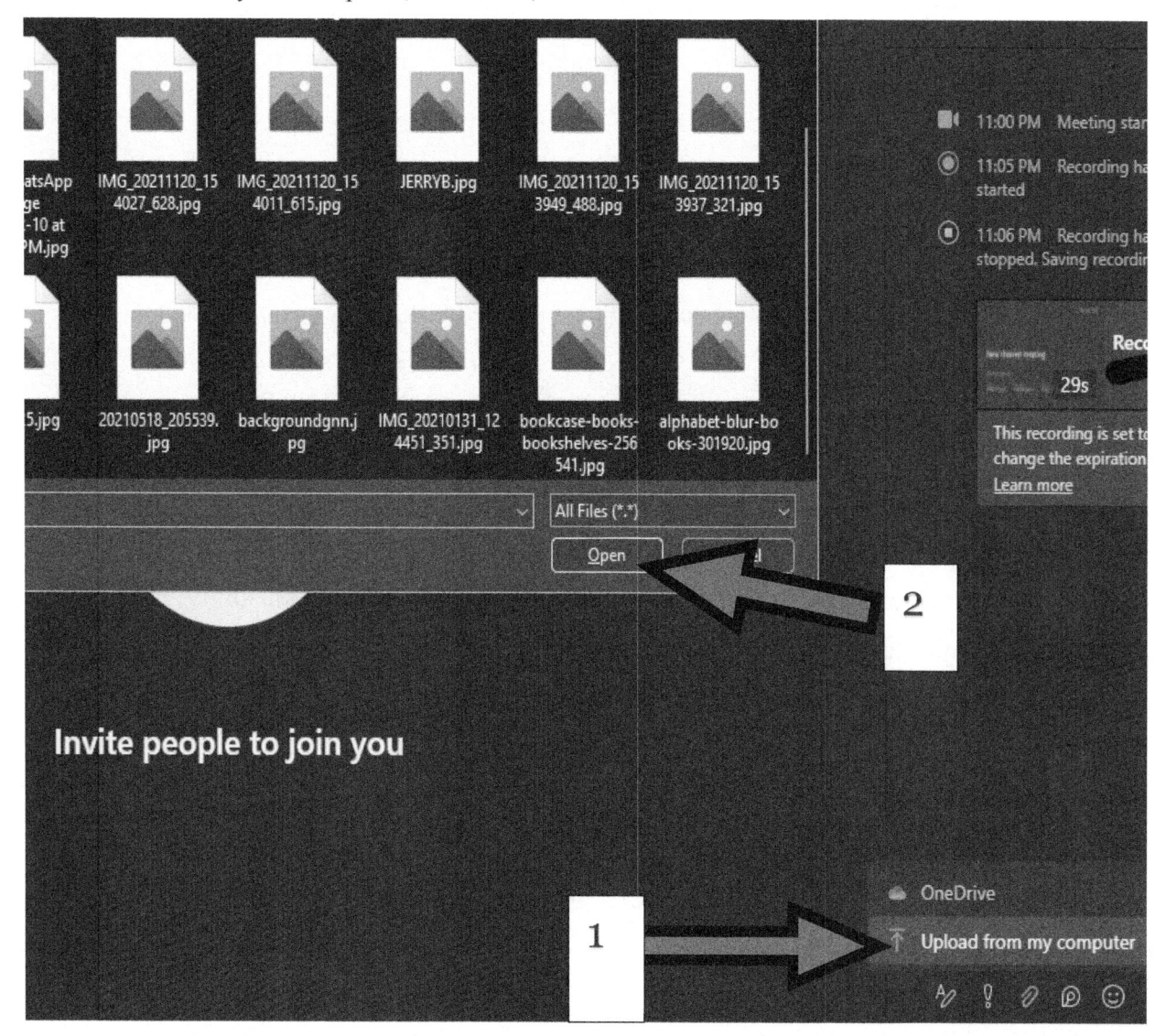

Step 5: Send the file

Once you've selected the file you want to share, click the "Send" button to send the file to your colleagues. They will receive a notification that a new file has been shared with them, and they can click on the link to open the file in Teams.

Chapter 4

Managing Tasks and Projects with Microsoft Teams

Microsoft Teams is a powerful collaboration tool that can help teams manage tasks and projects more efficiently. With Teams, you can create, assign, and track tasks, share files, communicate with team members, and collaborate in real-time. In this chapter, we'll explore how you can use Teams to manage tasks and projects, and some of the key features that can help you streamline your workflow.

Creating tasks and assigning them to team members

The capability of creating tasks and delegating them to specific members of a team is one of the most useful aspects of Microsoft Teams. This functionality helps to ensure that tasks are finished on time while also streamlining project management and improving accountability. In this piece, we'll discuss how to use Microsoft Teams' task creation and delegation features to delegate work to individual members of a team.

Developing an Assignment in Microsoft Teams

To begin the process of creating a task in Microsoft Teams, you will first need to launch the application and then head to the channel in which you want the task to be created. Once you've entered the channel, proceed with the following steps:

Step 1: You will need to click on the **plus sign** that is located to the right of the message box.

Step 2: From the dropdown menu, select "Task" to continue.

Step 3: Give the task a name and a description.

Step 4: Specify the nature of the work to be done (optional).

Step 5: Select a completion date for the assignment.

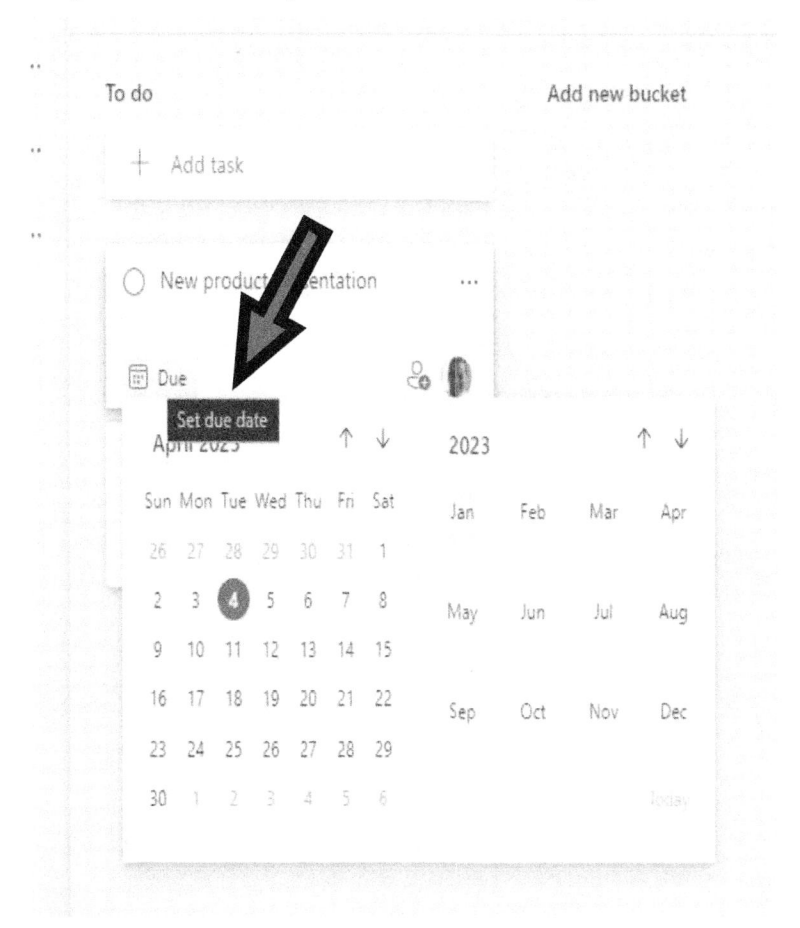

Step 6: Delegate the responsibility to a member of the team.

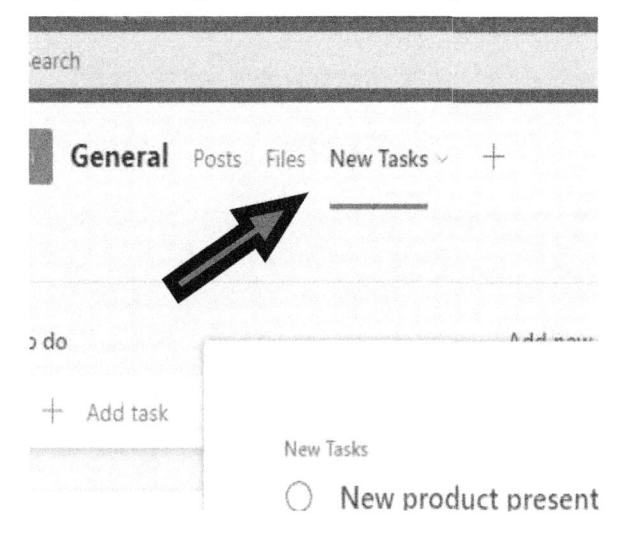

Step 7: Attach any relevant files or make any necessary comments.

Step 8: To save the task, click the "Create" button.

When you have finished creating a task, you will need to delegate it to a member of your team. This is the procedure to follow:

Step 1: Select the task you want to assign by clicking on it.

Step 2: Select the "Assign" button from the menu.

Step 3: Select the member of the team to whom you will delegate the responsibility for completing the task.

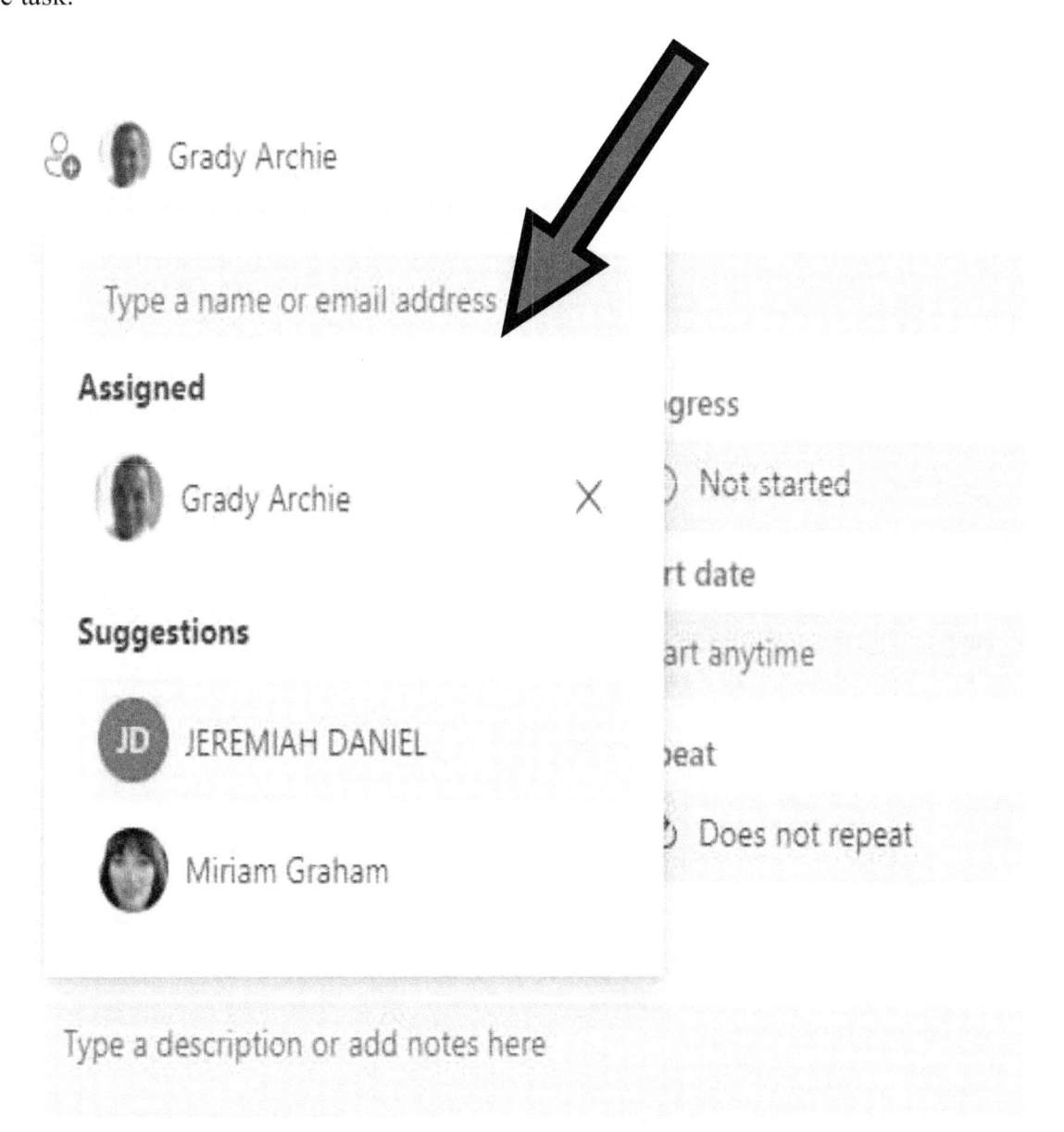

Step 4: To assign the task, click the "Save" button.

You can also delegate a task to multiple members of your team by selecting their names from a list of options that is presented to you.

Keeping Tabs on Your Work in Microsoft Teams

In Microsoft Teams, you are able to monitor the development of a task after you have first created and assigned it. In order to accomplish this, please follow these steps:

Step 1: In the channel where the task was initially created, navigate to the tab labeled "Tasks."

Step 2: Choose the activity that you want to keep track of.

Step 3: Examine the "Status" column to determine how far along the task you currently are.

Step 4: If additional information is required, comments or attachments can be added to the task.

Step 5: ensure that the status of the task is kept up to date as it is completed.

The members of a team can ensure that they are on the right track and that their work will be finished on time by checking the status of their tasks on a regular basis within Microsoft Teams.

Hints for Distributing Work in Microsoft Teams

The following are some pointers to consider when delegating tasks in Microsoft Teams:

- When delegating work to members of the team, make sure that everyone is aware of the expectations that have been set for them. This includes the extent of the task, the deadline, and any other information that is pertinent to the endeavor.
- Before delegating a task to a member of the team, it is important to take into account how busy they already are. Check to see that they have sufficient time to finish the task without becoming too overwhelmed by it.
- If members of your team are having difficulty completing a task, you should provide support and guidance for them. This might take the form of additional resources, training, or support on an individual basis.
- Make use of templates: If you find that you are frequently delegating the same kind of task, you should think about creating a template for it. This can result in time savings and a higher level of consistency.

- Check the status of the tasks on a regular basis to ensure that they are moving in the right direction and are not falling behind. This will assist you in identifying any problems at an early stage so that you can take corrective action, if required.

The Benefits of Delegating Work in Microsoft Teams

The process of delegating work in Microsoft Teams comes with a variety of benefits. Here are some examples:

- Increased personal responsibility Assigning tasks to members of a team helps increase personal responsibility by ensuring that individuals are aware of the responsibilities that are placed on their shoulders.
- Communication is made easier in Microsoft Teams thanks to the task-assignment feature, which consolidates all of the pertinent information into a single location.
- Increased collaboration is achieved through the process of task assignment, which motivates members of a team to cooperate and exchange information with one another.
- Greater visibility: Assigning tasks in Microsoft Teams provides greater visibility into the progress of projects. Team members can quickly and easily see what tasks need to be completed and the status of each task.
- Better time management: By assigning tasks with specific deadlines, team members can better manage their time and prioritize their work.
- Improved organization: Assigning tasks in Microsoft Teams helps to keep projects organized and ensures that tasks are not forgotten or overlooked.

Using the Planner app to manage projects

Microsoft Teams comes with a built-in app called Planner that can help you manage projects and tasks within your team. Planner provides a user-friendly interface for creating and tracking tasks, setting due dates, assigning tasks to team members, and monitoring progress. In this guide, we'll explore how to use the Planner app to manage projects on Microsoft Teams.

Creating a Plan in Planner

To create a plan in Planner, you'll need to navigate to the channel where you want to create the plan. Once you're in the channel, follow these steps:

Step 1: Click on the "+" sign to the right of the message box.

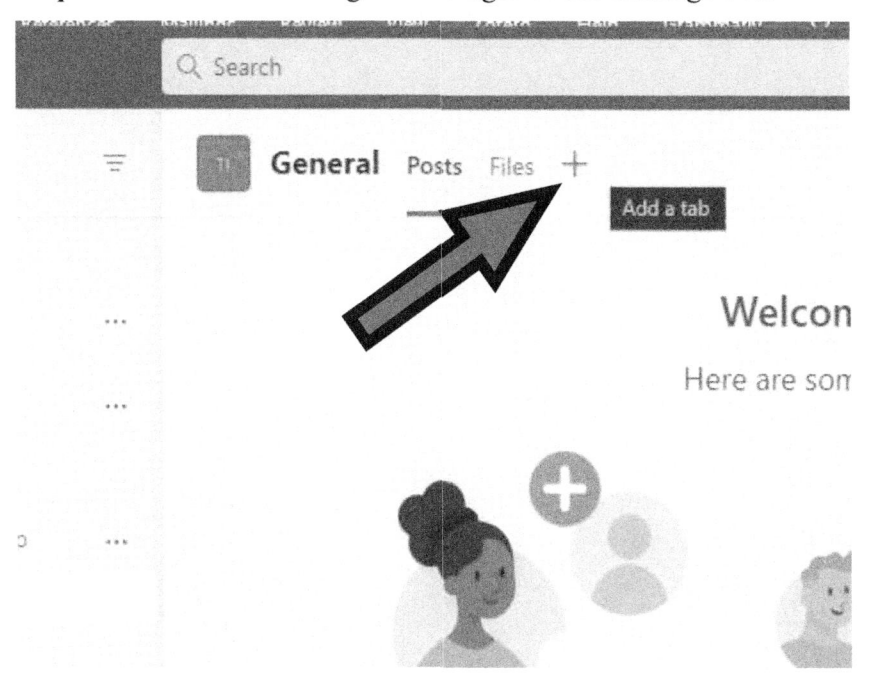

Step 2: Select "Planner" from the dropdown menu.

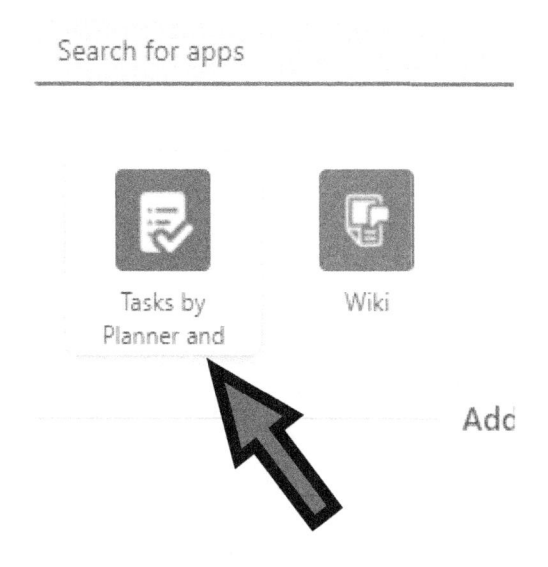

Step 3: Click on "Create a new plan."

Step 4: Give your plan a name and click "Save."

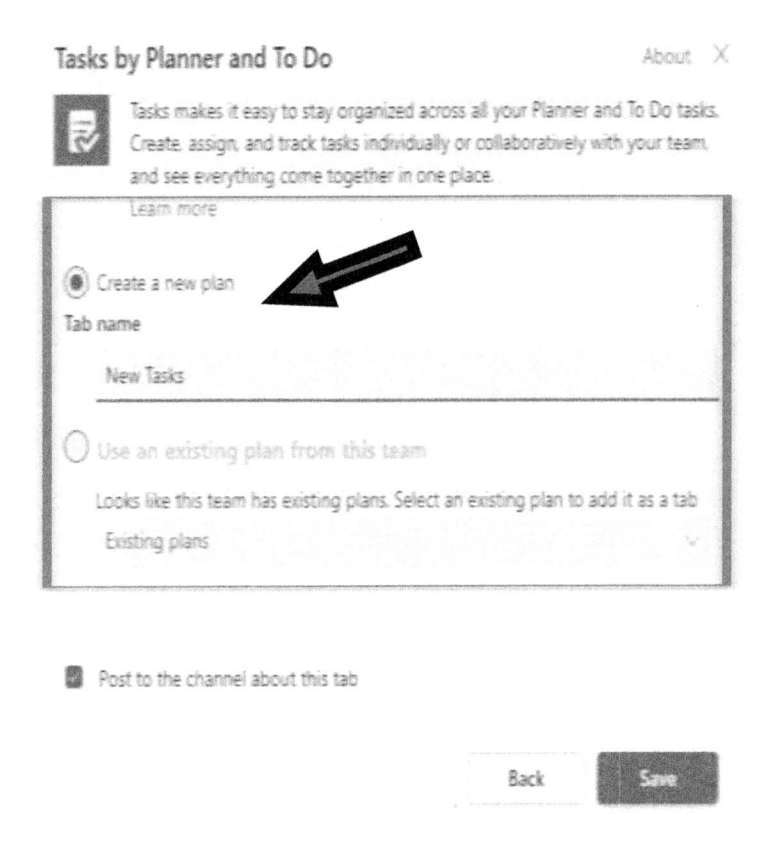

Your plan will now be created and you'll be taken to the plan's board view.

Creating Tasks in Planner

To create a task in Planner, follow these steps:

Step 1: Click on the "+" sign in the column where you want to add the task.

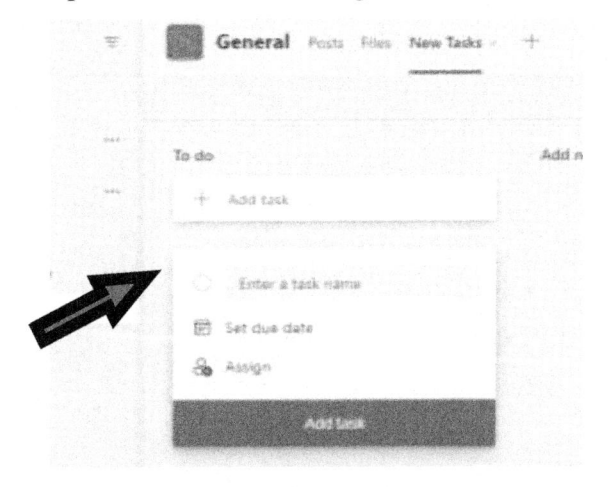

Step 2: Enter a title for the task.

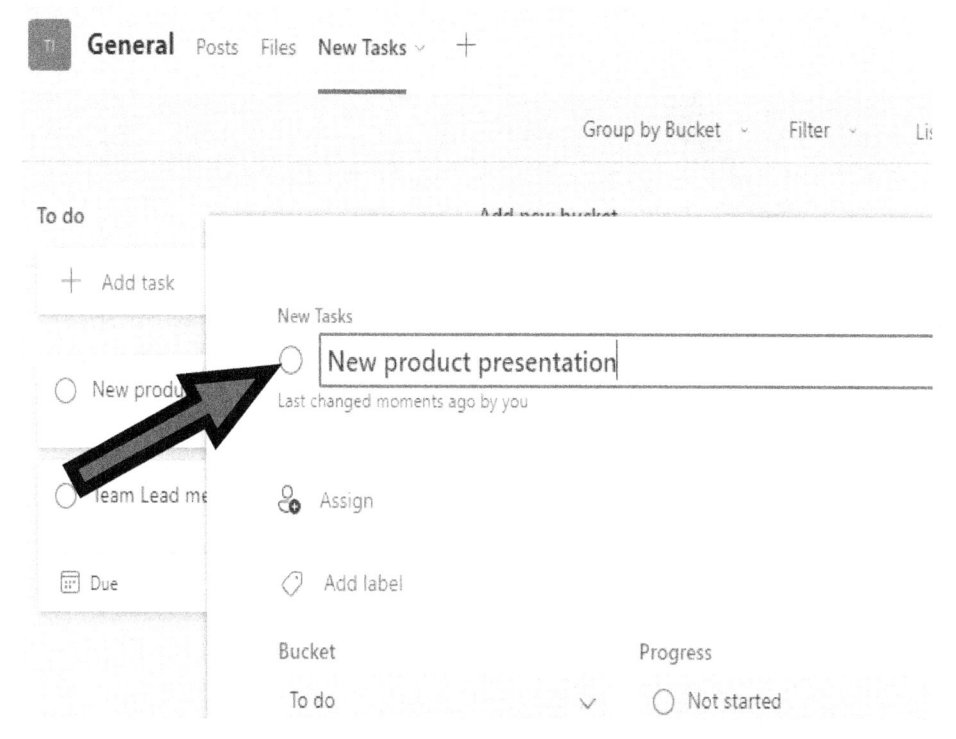

Step 3: Add a description of the task (optional).

Step 4: Assign the task to a team member by selecting their name from the dropdown menu.

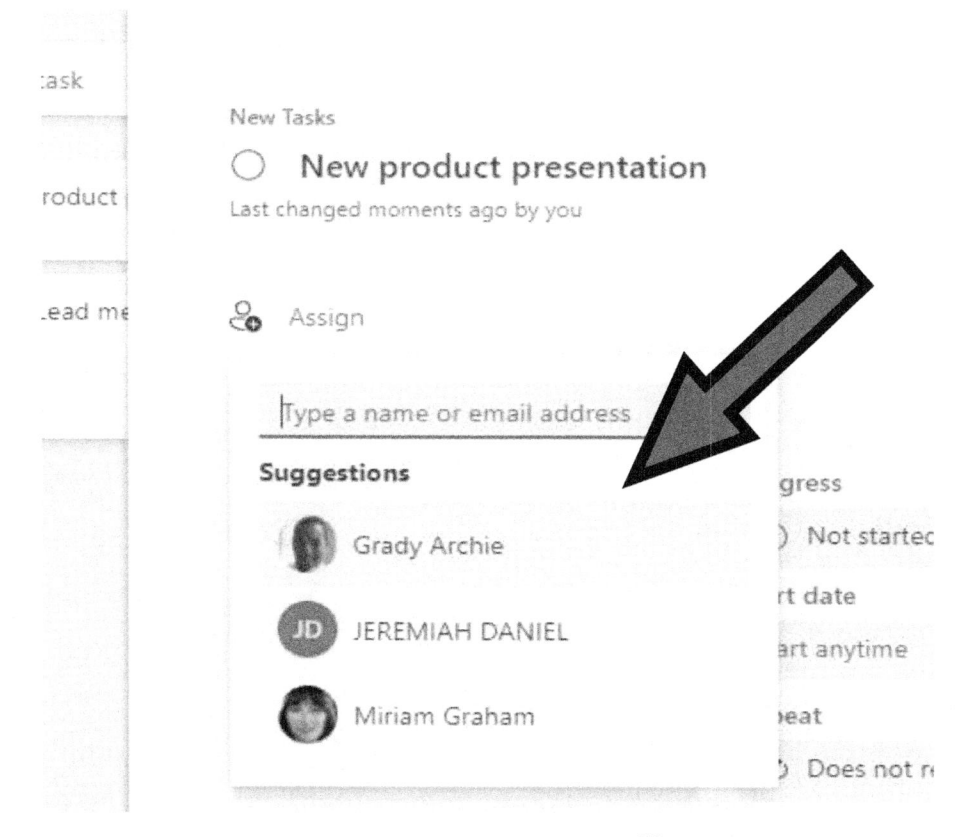

Step 5: Set a due date for the task.

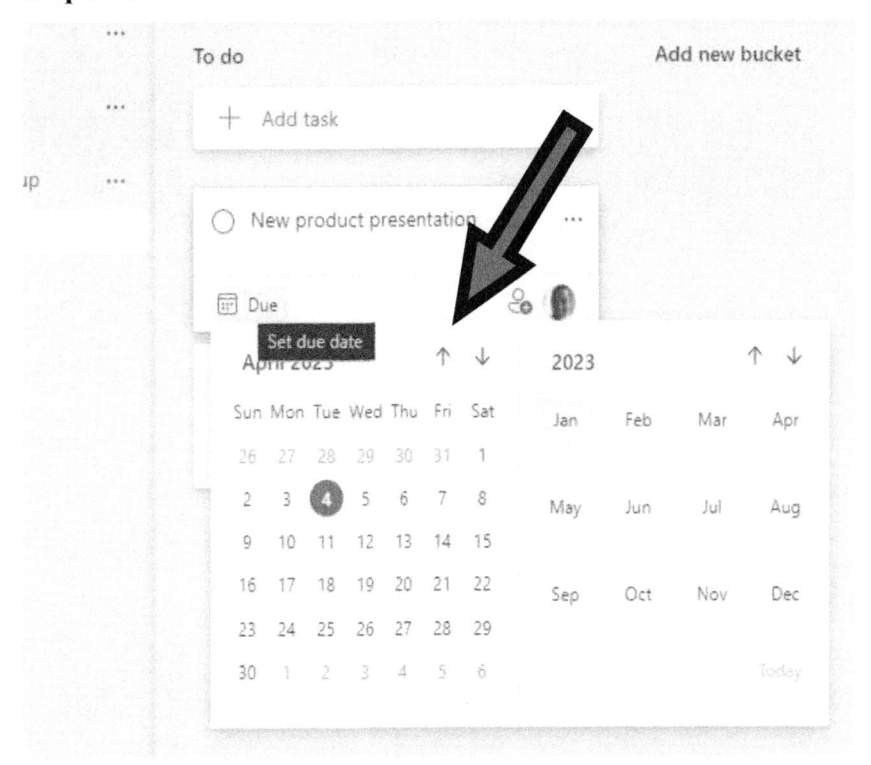

Step 6: Add any necessary attachments or comments.

Step 7: Click "Add task" to save the task.

Assigning Tasks in Planner

To assign a task in Planner, follow these steps:

Step 1: Click on the task you want to assign.

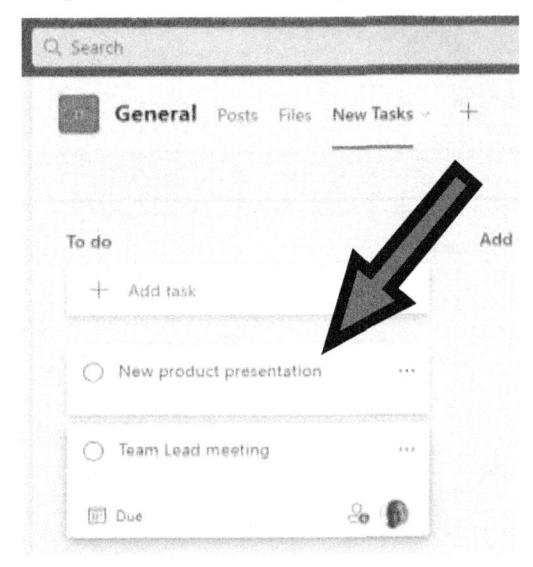

Step 2: Click on the "Assign" button.

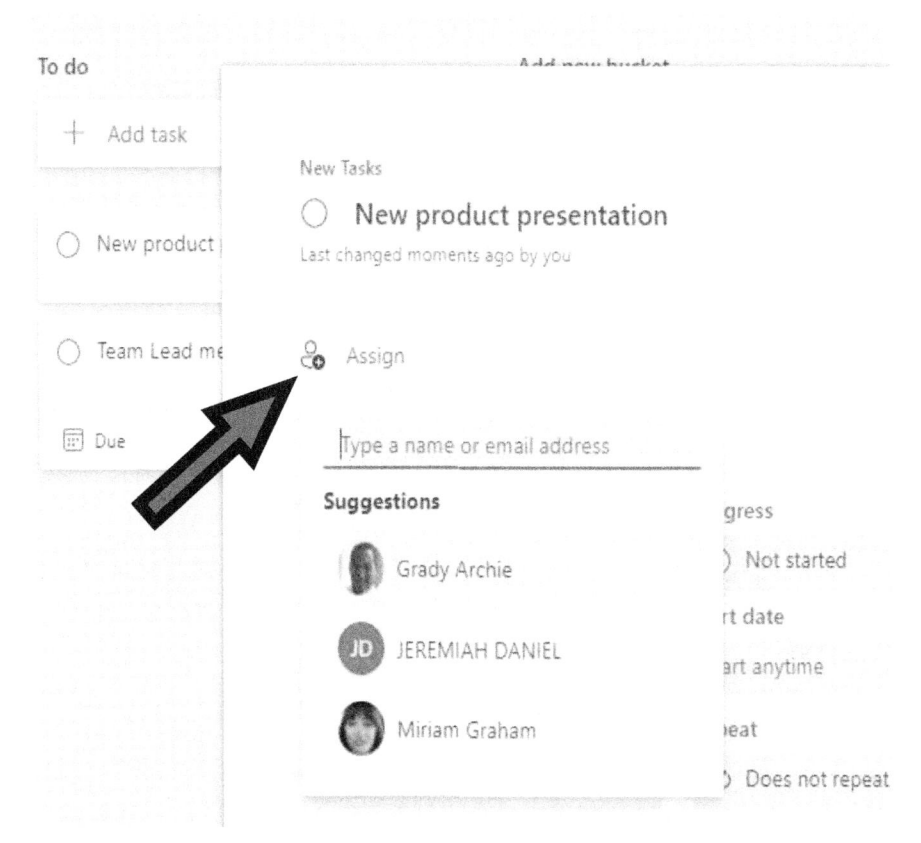

Step 3: Choose the team member you want to assign the task to.

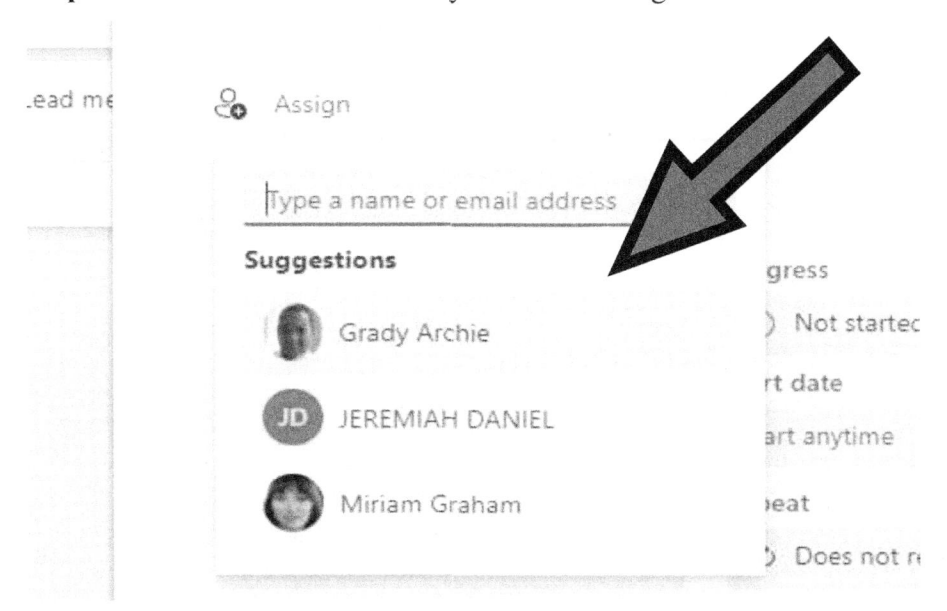

Step 4: Click "Save" to assign the task.

You can also assign a task to multiple team members by selecting them from the list of available options.

Tracking Progress in Planner

Once you've created and assigned tasks in Planner, you can track their progress by using the board view. The board view provides a visual representation of all the tasks in your plan, allowing you to see which tasks are completed, which ones are in progress, and which ones are yet to be started. To track progress in Planner, follow these steps:

Step 1: Navigate to the plan's board view.

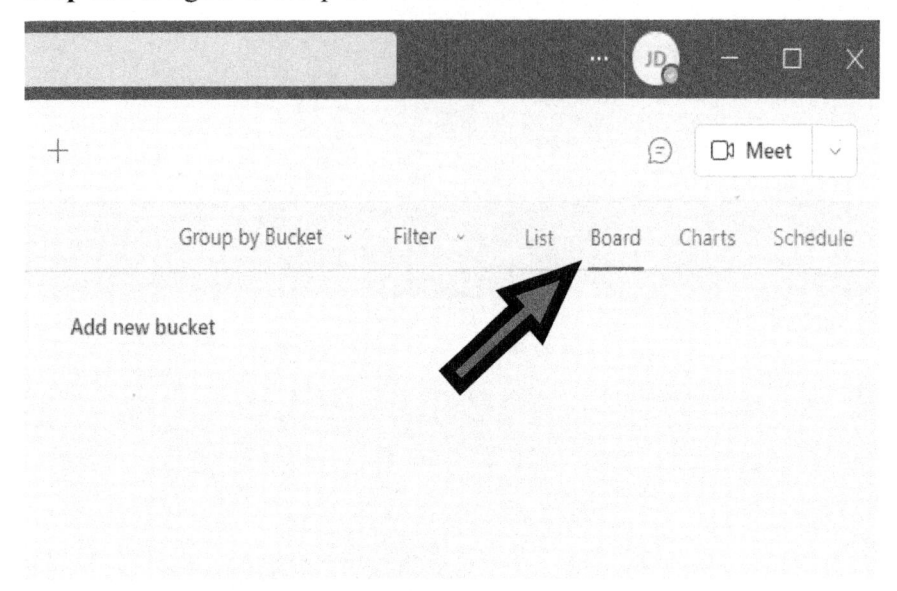

Step 2: Click and drag tasks between columns to update their status.

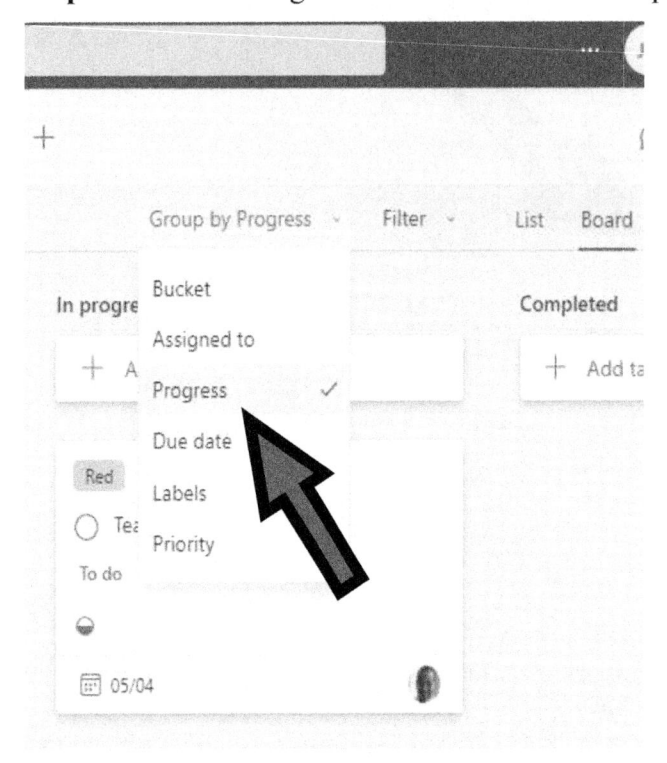

Step 3: Use the progress bar to see how much of the plan is completed.

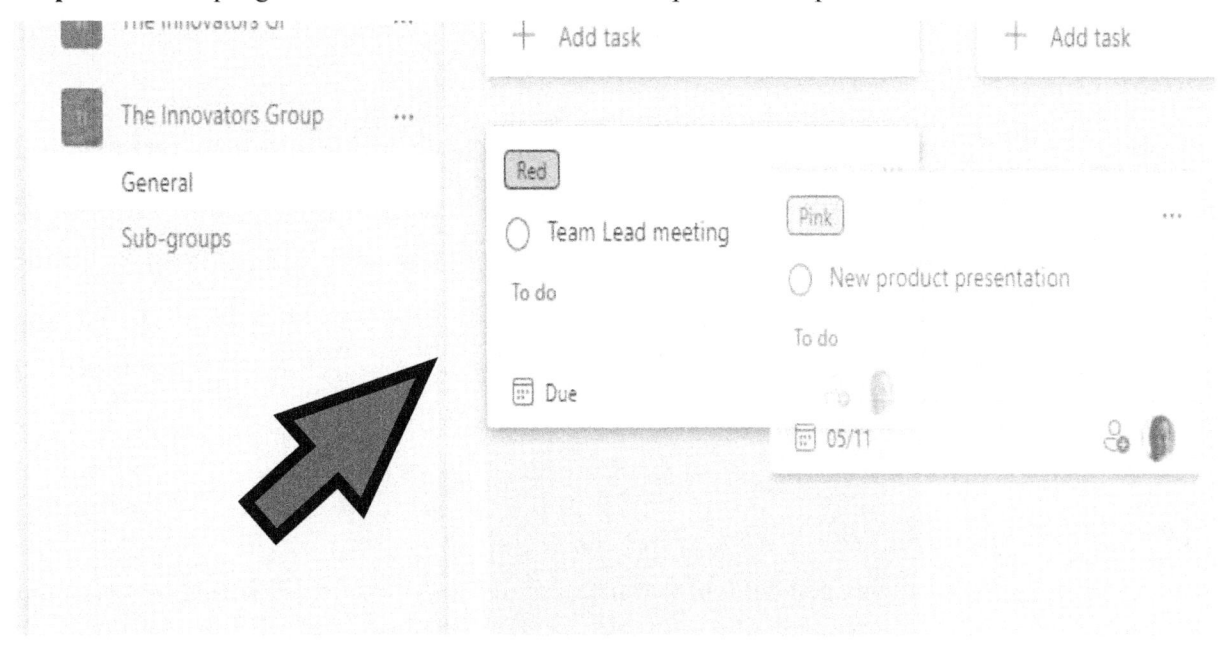

Step 4: Click on a task to see more details and make updates.

Tips for Managing Projects in Planner

Here are some tips for managing projects in Planner:
- Use buckets to organize tasks: Buckets allow you to group tasks by category or priority, making it easier to manage large projects.
- Set due dates for tasks: Setting due dates helps team members stay on track and ensures that tasks are completed on time.
- Use labels to categorize tasks: Labels allow you to categorize tasks by type, priority, or any other relevant criteria.
- Assign tasks to team members: Assigning tasks to team members ensures that everyone knows what they are responsible for and improves accountability.
- Use the checklist feature: The checklist feature allows you to break down tasks into smaller subtasks, making them more manageable and easier to complete.

Integrating Microsoft Teams with other project management tools

Microsoft Teams is a powerful collaboration tool that can be integrated with other project management tools to further streamline workflows, improve productivity, and increase efficiency. By integrating Teams with other project management tools, team members can access all the necessary information and tools in one place, reducing the need to switch between multiple applications. In this guide, we'll explore some of the most popular project management tools that can be integrated with Microsoft Teams.

Trello

Trello is a popular project management tool that uses boards, lists, and cards to organize tasks and projects. It can be integrated with Microsoft Teams, allowing team members to access Trello boards and cards directly from Teams. This integration can be especially useful for teams that use Trello for project management, as it eliminates the need to switch between multiple applications.

Asana

Asana is a project management tool that allows teams to track tasks and projects in real-time. When integrated with Microsoft Teams, Asana tasks can be accessed directly from Teams, and progress updates can be shared with team members in real-time. This integration can be especially useful for teams that use Asana for project management, as it allows them to easily access and manage their tasks without leaving Teams.

Jira

Jira is a popular project management tool used by software development teams to track issues, bugs, and feature requests. It can be integrated with Microsoft Teams, allowing team members to access Jira tickets directly from Teams. This integration can be especially useful for software development teams that use Jira for issue tracking, as it eliminates the need to switch between multiple applications.

GitHub

GitHub is a code hosting platform used by software development teams to collaborate on projects. When integrated with Microsoft Teams, team members can access GitHub repositories and issues directly from Teams. This integration can be especially useful for software development teams that use GitHub for version control and issue tracking, as it allows them to easily access and manage their code without leaving Teams.

Integrating Microsoft Teams with other project management tools can be a powerful way to streamline workflows, improve productivity, and increase efficiency. By providing a central location for managing tasks and projects, team members can access all the necessary information and tools in one place, reducing the need to switch between multiple applications. By exploring and utilizing these integrations, teams can better manage their projects, improve communication, and achieve better results.

Chapter 5

Using Microsoft Teams for Collaboration and Productivity

Collaborating on documents and presentations

Microsoft Teams offers a range of tools that enable teams to collaborate on documents and presentations in real-time. With Teams, team members can work together on the same document simultaneously, make edits, provide feedback, and share files. Here are some ways to collaborate on documents and presentations in Microsoft Teams:

Microsoft OneDrive integration: Microsoft Teams integrates seamlessly with OneDrive, allowing team members to easily access and share files. When collaborating on a document or presentation, store it in OneDrive and share it with the team through a Teams channel or chat. This way, everyone has access to the most up-to-date version of the file.

Real-time co-authoring: Teams enables real-time co-authoring on documents and presentations, which means that team members can work on the same document at the same time. As one person makes edits, the changes are visible to everyone else in real-time. This feature enables teams to work together efficiently and complete projects faster.

File sharing: Teams allows team members to easily share files with each other. You can share a document or presentation with a channel or chat, and team members can access it directly from Teams. Teams also supports file versioning, which means that previous versions of a file are saved, making it easy to revert to an earlier version if needed.

Comments and feedback: Teams allow team members to provide comments and feedback on documents and presentations. This feature enables collaboration and makes it easy to provide feedback and suggestions for improvement. Team members can reply to comments, and the entire conversation is saved, making it easy to follow up on feedback.

Integration with Microsoft Office: Teams integrates seamlessly with Microsoft Office, enabling teams to collaborate on Word, Excel, PowerPoint, and other Office documents directly from

Teams. This integration provides a comprehensive solution for document collaboration and ensures that everyone is working on the same version of the document.

Using the OneNote app for note-taking and sharing

OneNote is a digital notebook that enables users to take and organize notes, create to-do lists, and collaborate with others in real-time. Here are some ways to use the OneNote app on Microsoft Teams:

- **Create a OneNote notebook**: Teams allows you to create a OneNote notebook directly from the Teams interface. Simply click on the "+" sign in a channel or chat, select "OneNote", and choose "Notebook" to create a new notebook. You can then share the notebook with team members, enabling them to view and edit the notes.

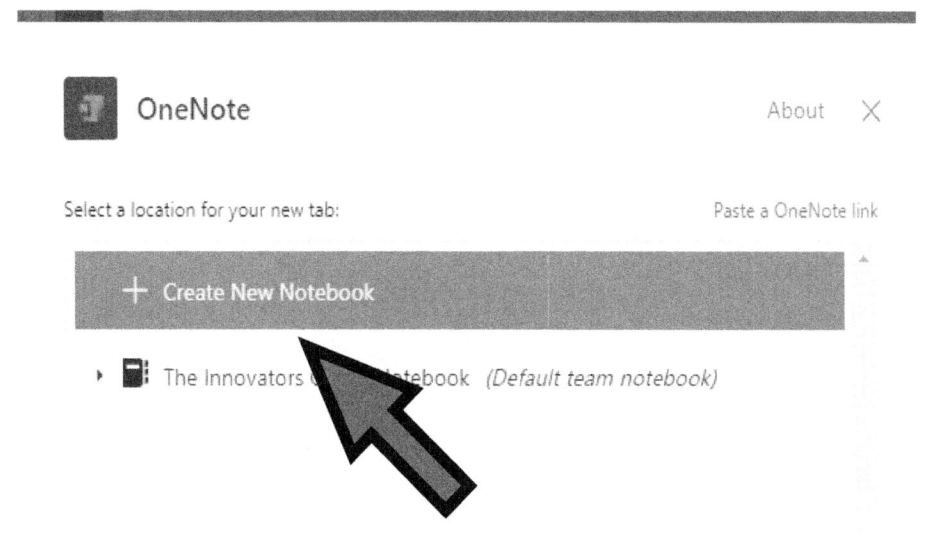

- **Share notes and collaborate in real-time**: Once you've created a OneNote notebook, you can share it with team members, enabling them to collaborate on notes and make changes in real-time. This feature allows teams to work together efficiently and ensures that everyone is working on the same version of the notes.

- **Organize notes with sections and pages**: OneNote allows users to organize notes with sections and pages, making it easy to find the information you need quickly. You can create sections for different topics or projects, and pages for specific notes or tasks. This organization helps to keep notes tidy and makes it easier to collaborate with others.

- **Use tags and labels**: OneNote allows you to add tags and labels to notes, making it easy to find and organize information. You can use tags to mark important notes or tasks, or to indicate the status of a project. This feature helps to keep notes organized and makes it easier to collaborate with others.
- **Access notes from anywhere**: OneNote syncs automatically with the cloud, enabling users to access notes from anywhere, on any device. This feature is particularly useful for teams working remotely or on-the-go, as it allows them to stay up-to-date with the latest information and collaborate with others in real-time.

Chapter 6

Security and Privacy in Microsoft Teams

Security and privacy are critical considerations when using any collaboration platform, including Microsoft Teams. Microsoft Teams provides a range of security and privacy features to protect user data and ensure compliance with data protection regulations. Some of the key security and privacy features in Microsoft Teams include:

- Data encryption: Teams uses end-to-end encryption to protect user data, ensuring that messages, files, and calls are secure and cannot be intercepted by unauthorized users.
- Multi-factor authentication: Teams supports multi-factor authentication, requiring users to provide additional verification when logging in to their accounts. This feature provides an extra layer of security, helping to prevent unauthorized access to user data.
- Role-based access control: Teams supports role-based access control, enabling administrators to control access to sensitive data and features. This feature ensures that only authorized users can access confidential information.
- Compliance and regulatory support: Teams is designed to comply with a range of regulatory frameworks, including GDPR, HIPAA, and ISO 27001. This ensures that user data is handled in accordance with data protection regulations, protecting user privacy and data security.
- Privacy controls: Teams provides users with a range of privacy controls, allowing them to control who can see their profile information, status, and activities. Users can also choose to make their conversations private, preventing others from accessing their messages or files.

Protecting sensitive data and files

Protecting sensitive data and files is crucial for organizations using Microsoft Teams. Microsoft Teams provides several built-in features to help protect sensitive data and files, ensuring that they remain secure and accessible only to authorized users. Here are some ways to protect sensitive data and files on Microsoft Teams:

- **Use data loss prevention (DLP) policies**: DLP policies are used to identify and protect sensitive data from being shared outside the organization. Teams offers DLP policies that allow administrators to define rules that block or restrict the sharing of sensitive information. For example, organizations can use DLP policies to prevent users from sharing confidential information such as credit card numbers, social security numbers, or other personally identifiable information (PII).
- **Use sensitivity labels**: Sensitivity labels are used to classify and protect sensitive files and data. They can be applied to individual files or entire Teams channels, and they help ensure that sensitive data is accessible only to authorized users. Sensitivity labels can also be used to enforce DLP policies and control access to sensitive information.
- **Implement access controls**: Teams provides a range of access controls that allow administrators to control who has access to sensitive data and files. This includes controlling access to Teams channels, files, and folders, as well as setting permissions for individual users. By implementing access controls, organizations can ensure that sensitive data is only accessible to authorized users.
- **Use encryption**: Teams uses end-to-end encryption to protect messages and files from unauthorized access. Encryption ensures that data is secure while in transit and at rest, helping to prevent data breaches and unauthorized access.
- **Use secure storage solutions**: Teams provides integration with Microsoft OneDrive and SharePoint for secure file storage. These platforms offer advanced security features such as encryption, access controls, and backup and recovery options, ensuring that sensitive files are stored securely and accessible only to authorized users.

Protecting sensitive data and files on Microsoft Teams is crucial for maintaining the security and privacy of organizational data. By implementing DLP policies, sensitivity labels, access controls, encryption, and secure storage solutions, organizations can ensure that sensitive data is accessible only to authorized users and protected from unauthorized access or data breaches.

Ensuring privacy and compliance with regulations

Ensuring privacy and compliance with regulations is a critical aspect of using Microsoft Teams. Organizations must adhere to various regulations and privacy laws, such as the General Data

Protection Regulation (GDPR) and the Health Insurance Portability and Accountability Act (HIPAA). Here are some ways to ensure privacy and compliance with regulations in Microsoft Teams:

- **Use privacy settings**: Microsoft Teams provides several privacy settings that allow administrators to control how data is used and shared. For example, administrators can control whether users can edit or delete messages, whether users can see each other's presence status, and whether users can search for content in Teams.

- **Enable retention policies**: Retention policies help ensure that data is retained or deleted according to regulatory requirements. Teams provides retention policies that allow administrators to define rules for retaining or deleting data, including messages, files, and chats.
- **Use eDiscovery**: eDiscovery allows organizations to identify, collect, and preserve electronic data for legal purposes. Teams provides eDiscovery capabilities that allow administrators to search and export data across Teams, Exchange, and SharePoint.

- **Implement third-party compliance solutions**: Microsoft Teams integrates with various third-party compliance solutions that help ensure regulatory compliance. These solutions can provide additional features, such as monitoring and reporting, to help ensure that data is being handled in compliance with regulations.
- **Educate users**: Educating users on privacy and compliance is crucial for maintaining privacy and compliance with regulations. Organizations should provide regular training and education to users on how to handle sensitive data and how to use Teams in a compliant manner.
- **Monitor and audit activity**: Monitoring and auditing activity in Teams can help detect and prevent unauthorized access or data breaches. Teams provides audit logs that allow administrators to track user activity, including logins, file access, and message activity.

Chapter 7

Customizing Microsoft Teams for Your Organization

Customizing themes and branding in Microsoft Teams is a crucial aspect of enhancing organizational identity and communication. While Teams provides several pre-built themes, these may not align with an organization's branding or color scheme. Creating a custom theme allows an organization to align its Teams environment with its branding and color scheme.

Customizing themes in Teams involves selecting a primary color and adjusting the theme's contrast and saturation settings to suit the organization's style. This can help create a cohesive look and feel across an organization's various communication and collaboration channels. By creating a custom theme, an organization can ensure that its Teams environment matches its logo, website, or other marketing materials. The same theme can also be used across all Microsoft 365 applications to maintain consistency throughout the organization.

Customizing branding in Teams involves changing the logo, background image, and other visual elements to align with an organization's identity and style. This helps create a professional and consistent look and feel across all communication and collaboration channels. When an organization customizes its branding in Teams, it can create a cohesive experience for employees and external partners.

Customizing themes and branding

One of the features that make Teams so popular is the ability to customize it to suit the needs of different organizations. Customization is crucial to ensuring that Teams meets the specific needs of a business, from branding and appearance to functionality and integration.

In this section, we will explore how to customize the themes and branding of Microsoft Teams to align with your organization's identity and style. We will cover the different customization options available, how to create custom themes, and best practices for branding your Teams environment.

Importance on customizing in Microsoft Teams

While the out-of-the-box features and functionalities of Teams are impressive, every organization has unique needs and requirements. This is where customization becomes essential. Customizing

Microsoft Teams allows organizations to tailor the platform to their specific needs, making it more effective and efficient for their teams.

There are several reasons why customizing Microsoft Teams is important for organizations:

- Enhancing the User Experience: By customizing Teams, organizations can create a more personalized and intuitive user experience. This can include creating custom channels and tabs, setting up automated workflows, and integrating with other applications. When Teams is tailored to the needs of the organization, team members can work more efficiently and effectively.
- Branding Consistency: Consistent branding is crucial for creating a professional and cohesive image for your organization. Customizing Teams with your organization's branding, including colors, logo, and background images, helps create a consistent and recognizable look and feel across all your communication and collaboration channels. This can help build trust and familiarity with clients, customers, and partners.
- Improved Communication: Customizing Teams can also enhance communication within an organization. By creating custom channels, teams can collaborate and share information in a way that aligns with their specific workflows and processes. This can help streamline communication, reducing the risk of miscommunication and increasing the speed of decision-making.
- Increased Productivity: When Teams is customized to meet the needs of an organization, team members can work more productively. This can include setting up automated workflows, creating custom policies and governance rules, and integrating with other applications. By automating routine tasks and streamlining workflows, teams can focus on more strategic and value-adding activities.
- Improved Security and Compliance: Customizing Teams can also improve security and compliance within an organization. This can include setting up custom policies for access control and data retention, ensuring that sensitive information is protected and compliance regulations are met. This can help reduce the risk of data breaches and legal issues.

Customizing Themes in Microsoft Teams:

Microsoft Teams offers a variety of pre-built themes, including light, dark, and high contrast themes. While these themes may be sufficient for some organizations, others may want to create custom themes that align with their brand and color scheme. Customizing themes in Microsoft

Teams allows organizations to create a cohesive look and feel across all their communication and collaboration channels.

You need to log in to Microsoft Admin Center to get the ability to perform these steps:
- Click on your profile picture in the top-right corner of the Teams window and select "Settings."
- In the "Settings" window, select "General" from the left-hand menu.
- Under the "Theme" option, click on "Custom" to create a new custom theme.
- In the "Custom theme" window, select a primary color for the theme. Teams will generate secondary colors automatically based on your selection.
- Adjust the theme's contrast and saturation settings to your liking.
- Once you have created your custom theme, click "Save" to apply it.

Creating a custom theme allows organizations to align their Teams environment with their brand and color scheme. This creates a consistent and professional look across all communication and collaboration channels. Custom themes can match a company's logo, website, or other marketing materials, helping to reinforce the organization's brand identity.

In addition to aligning with an organization's brand identity, custom themes can also improve usability. A custom theme can make important buttons and icons stand out, improving navigation and usability for users. Additionally, custom themes can help reduce eye strain by using colors that are easy on the eyes.

Customizing Branding in Microsoft Teams:

Customizing the branding of your Teams environment involves changing the logo, background image, and other visual elements to align with your organization's identity and style. This helps create a cohesive look and feel across your organization's various communication and collaboration channels.

To customize the branding of your Teams environment, follow these steps:
- Sign in to the Microsoft Teams Admin Center as an admin user.
- In the left-hand menu, select "Teams" and then "Upgrade" to access the "Upgrade settings" page.
- In the "Upgrade settings" page, scroll down to the "Custom messaging" section.
- Upload your organization's logo and set a custom background image for the Teams sign-in page.

- Save your changes.
- By customizing the branding of your Teams environment, you can create a professional and consistent look and feel across all your communication and collaboration channels.

Best Practices for Branding in Microsoft Teams:

When branding your Microsoft Teams environment, there are a few best practices to keep in mind to ensure consistency and effectiveness:

- **Use your organization's primary colors**: Use the same colors across your Teams environment that you use in your other marketing and branding materials to maintain consistency.
- **Use a high-quality logo**: Ensure that the logo you use is of high quality and meets the size requirements for Teams. This helps create a professional and polished look for your Teams environment.
- **Use a custom background image**: Use a custom background image that aligns with your organization's branding and style. This can be an image of your company's headquarters or a branded image that conveys your company's values.
- **Be consistent**: Ensure that your branding is consistent across all your Microsoft 365 applications, including Teams. This helps create a cohesive look and feel for your organization.

Uploading organization logo and background image

Uploading organization logo and background image on Microsoft Teams is a crucial step in customizing the branding of the platform to align with your organization's identity and style. It helps create a consistent look and feel across all your communication and collaboration channels, making it easier for users to identify with your organization and its values.

In this section, we will explore the steps to customize the branding of your Teams environment by uploading your organization's logo and background image.

Accessing Microsoft Teams Admin Center

To access the Microsoft Teams Admin Center, you must have admin user credentials. Once you have signed in, follow these steps:

- In the left-hand menu, select "Teams."
- Click on "Upgrade" to access the "Upgrade settings" page.

Uploading Organization Logo:

Once you have accessed the "Upgrade settings" page, follow these steps to upload your organization's logo

- In the "Custom messaging" section, click on "Change" next to the "Logo" option.
- In the "Upload logo" window, select the image file you want to use as your organization's logo.

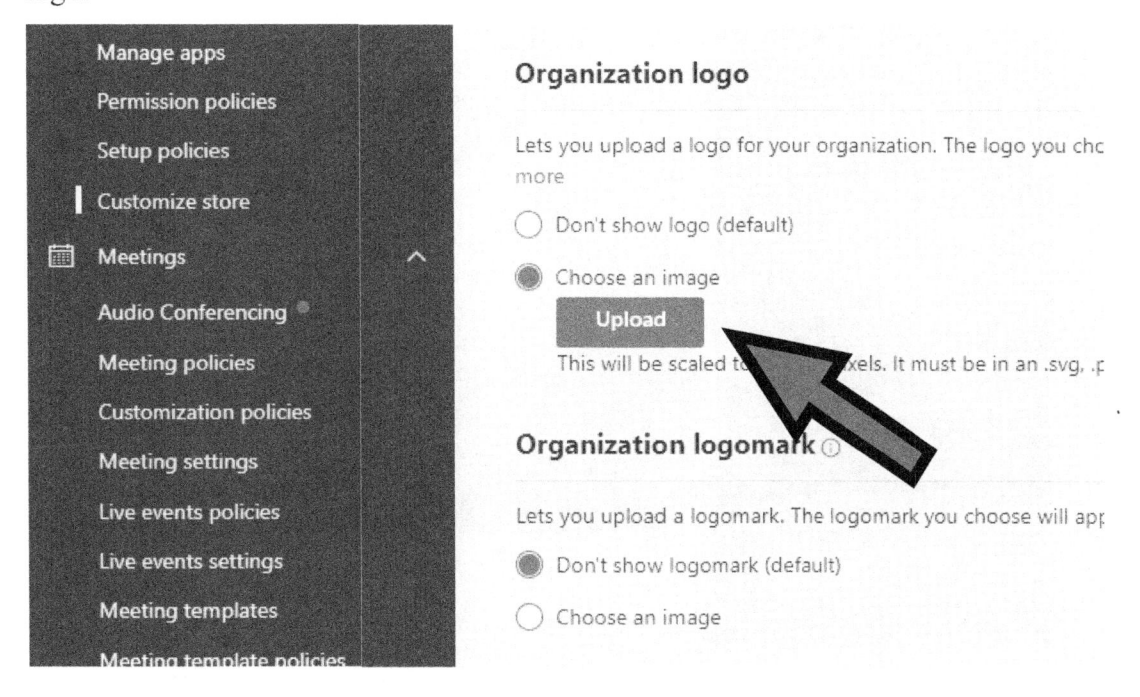

- Crop the image to fit within the recommended dimensions.
- Click "Save" to upload the logo.

Teams will automatically resize your logo to fit within the platform's parameters. However, it is important to ensure that the logo you upload is of high quality and meets the size requirements for Teams to ensure a professional and polished look for your Teams environment.

Uploading Background Image:

To customize the background image on the Teams sign-in page, follow these steps:

- In the "Custom messaging" section, click on "Change" next to the "Background image" option.

- In the "Upload background image" window, select the image file you want to use as your organization's background image.

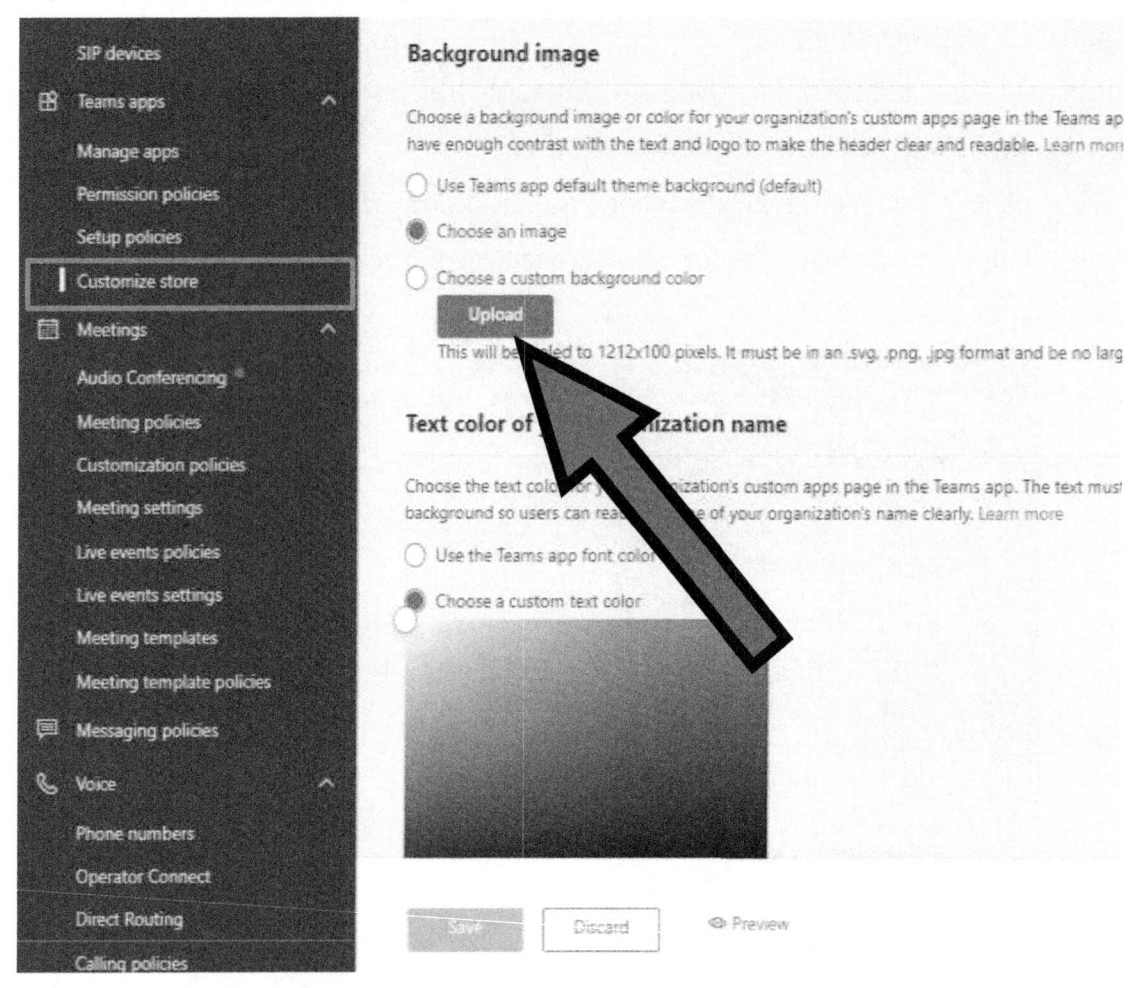

- Crop the image to fit within the recommended dimensions.
- Click "Save" to upload the background image.

The background image can be an image of your company's headquarters or a branded image that conveys your company's values. It is essential to ensure that the image you upload aligns with your organization's branding and style to create a cohesive look and feel across all your communication and collaboration channels.

Best Practices for Uploading Logo and Background Image:
When uploading your organization's logo and background image on Microsoft Teams, it is important to follow some best practices to ensure consistency and effectiveness:

- **Use high-quality images**: Ensure that the images you upload are of high quality and meet the size requirements for Teams. This helps create a professional and polished look for your Teams environment.
- **Use images that align with your branding and style**: Use images that align with your organization's branding and style to create a cohesive look and feel across all your communication and collaboration channels.
- **Keep it simple**: Avoid using complex images or backgrounds that may distract users or make it difficult for them to navigate the platform.
- **Ensure contrast and visibility**: Ensure that the images you upload have sufficient contrast and visibility to make it easy for users to read text or navigate the platform.

Creating custom workflows and automations

Creating custom workflows and automations in Microsoft Teams is an excellent way to streamline processes, save time, and improve efficiency. Teams' integration with Microsoft Power Automate allows users to create automated workflows that connect Teams with other Microsoft 365 applications, third-party applications, and services.

In this section, we will explore the steps to create custom workflows and automations in Microsoft Teams.

Step 1: Choose a Trigger

The first step in creating a custom workflow is choosing a trigger. A trigger is an event that starts the workflow. In Teams, triggers can include new messages, new channel messages, new team members, or any other Teams-related event.

Step 2: Choose an Action

After choosing the trigger, the next step is to choose an action. An action is a task that you want the workflow to perform when the trigger event occurs. In Teams, actions can include sending messages, creating channels, adding members, or any other Teams-related action.

Step 3: Configure the Workflow

Once you have chosen the trigger and action, the next step is to configure the workflow. This involves setting up the parameters of the trigger and action, as well as any additional steps or conditions that you want to include in the workflow.

For example, you can configure a workflow to send a message to a specific channel whenever a new member joins a team. You can also add conditions that check if the new member is part of a specific department or team and send different messages based on the condition.

Step 4: Test and Launch the Workflow

After configuring the workflow, it is important to test it before launching it. This allows you to identify and fix any issues before the workflow is implemented.

Once you have tested the workflow, you can launch it. The workflow will then run automatically whenever the trigger event occurs, performing the specified action and any additional steps or conditions that you have included.

Create a flow from the message menu in Microsoft Teams

Microsoft Teams users can also create manually triggered flows from the overflow menu of a Microsoft Teams message.

Follow these steps to create a manually triggered flow from the Microsoft Teams store

1. Sign into Microsoft Teams.
2. Select the ellipses (…) menu of any message in Teams.

3. Select **More actions**.

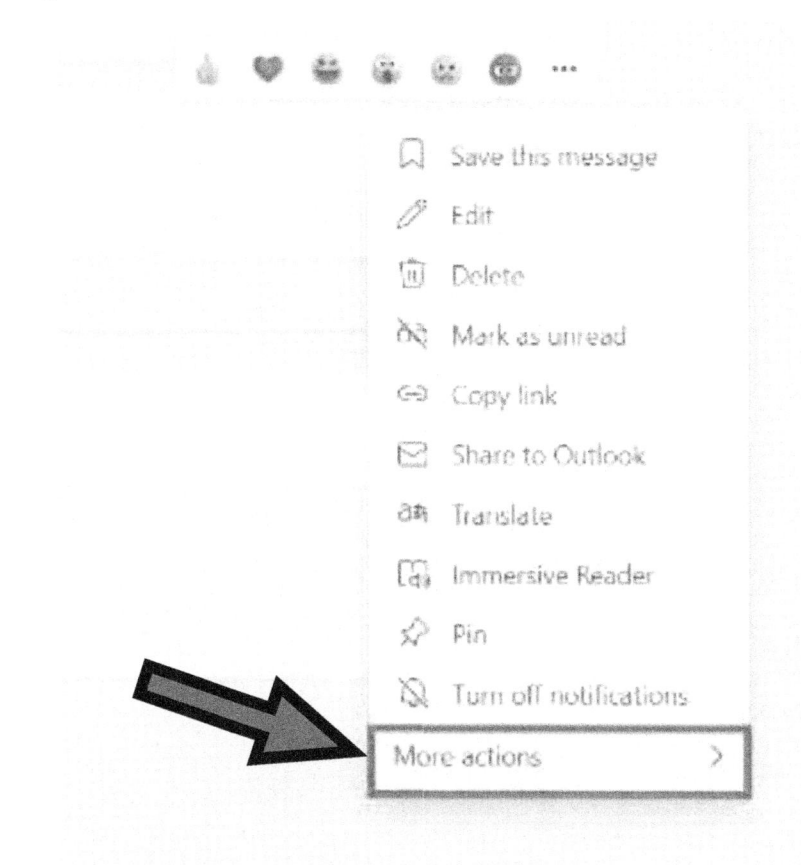

4. Select **Create new action**.

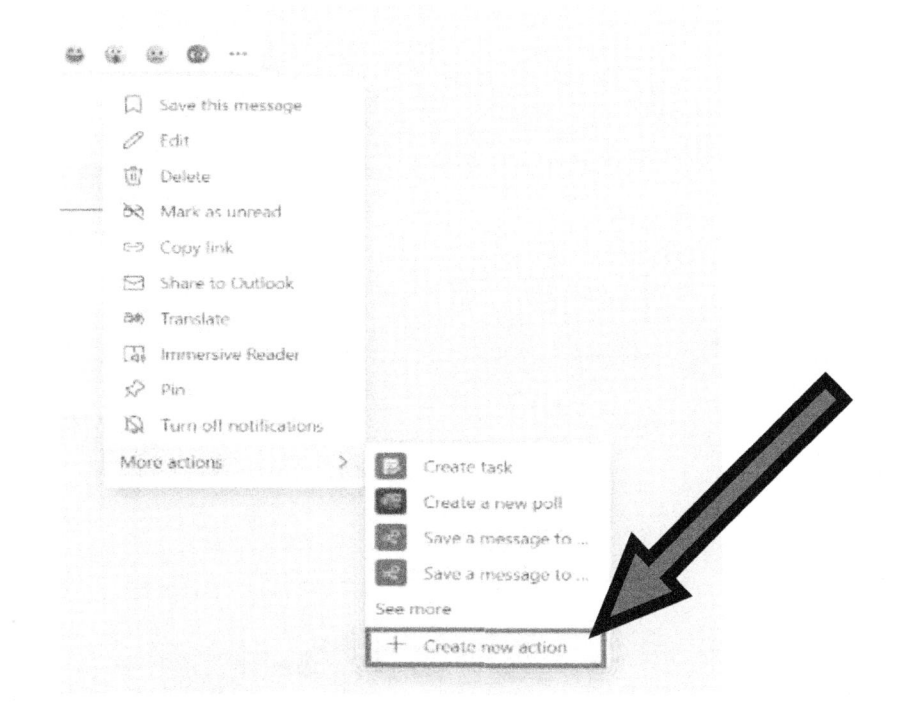

You now see list of templates that use the **for a selected message** manual trigger.

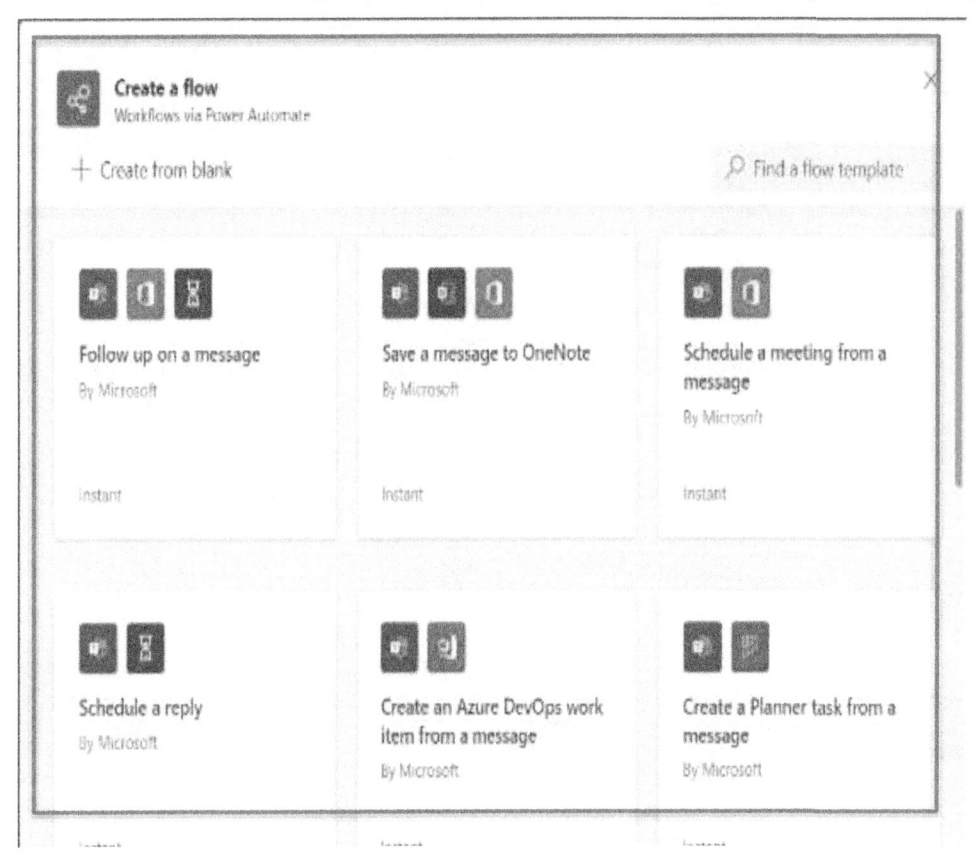

5. Select any template to set up the connections you need.

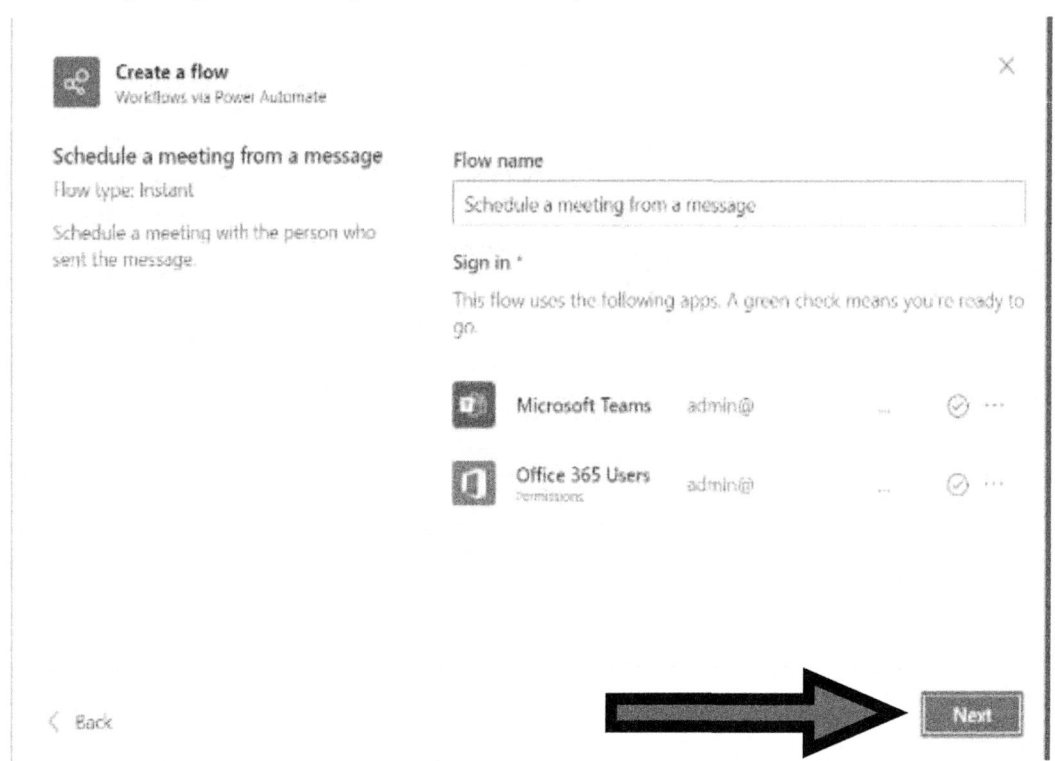

6. Select **Next** to setup the parameters that the template needs.

7. You will see a confirmation page once your flow is created successfully.

Benefits of Custom Workflows and Automations

Creating custom workflows and automations in Microsoft Teams can provide numerous benefits to organizations, including:

- Improved efficiency: By automating tasks and processes, workflows can save time and improve efficiency, allowing users to focus on more important tasks.
- Enhanced communication and collaboration: Workflows can help improve communication and collaboration within teams by providing automatic notifications and reminders, as well as facilitating the sharing of information and data.
- Reduced errors and inconsistencies: Workflows can help reduce errors and inconsistencies by automating repetitive tasks and ensuring that all tasks are completed consistently and accurately.
- Better tracking and reporting: Workflows can provide better tracking and reporting capabilities by automatically logging all events and actions, as well as providing real-time updates and alerts.

Creating custom workflows and automations in Microsoft Teams can help organizations save time, improve efficiency, and enhance communication and collaboration. By following the steps outlined above and leveraging the power of Microsoft Power Automate, users can easily create custom workflows and automations that connect Teams with other Microsoft 365 applications, third-party applications, and services. With the benefits of improved efficiency, enhanced communication and collaboration, reduced errors and inconsistencies, and better tracking and reporting, custom workflows and automations are an essential tool for any organization looking to streamline processes and improve productivity.

Chapter 8

Troubleshooting Common Issues in Microsoft Teams

In today's digital age, technology is an essential component of both personal and professional life. One of the most widely used communication and collaboration platforms is Microsoft Teams, which offers a wide range of features such as instant messaging, file sharing, video conferencing, and more. However, like any other technology, Teams is also prone to glitches and errors that can significantly impact productivity and collaboration.

Troubleshooting common issues in Microsoft Teams is crucial for ensuring that the platform functions smoothly, and team members can collaborate without any disruptions. Let's explore why troubleshooting is so important and the benefits it offers.

- **Increased Productivity:** When common issues such as slow internet connectivity or poor audio and video quality are not addressed promptly, they can severely hamper team productivity. For instance, if a team member is unable to join a meeting due to connectivity issues, the entire team's progress can be affected. However, by troubleshooting such problems promptly, teams can continue working efficiently, leading to improved productivity.

- **Improved Communication:** Effective communication is the key to successful collaboration, and Microsoft Teams provides multiple channels for team members to communicate. However, when communication channels such as chat, file sharing, or video conferencing are not functioning correctly, it can create confusion and delay in decision-making. Troubleshooting these issues ensures that communication channels are working correctly and team members can communicate seamlessly.

- **Enhances User Experience:** A positive user experience is crucial for the adoption and success of any technology. Troubleshooting common issues ensures that users have a smooth experience while using Teams. This, in turn, increases user satisfaction and encourages them to continue using Teams as their primary communication and collaboration platform.

- **Saves Time and Money:** When teams face common issues such as lost files or messages, it can be time-consuming to recreate them, leading to a loss of valuable time. Additionally, if these issues occur frequently, it can result in increased costs associated with lost productivity and missed deadlines. Troubleshooting common issues promptly can help teams save time and money by addressing issues before they escalate.
- **Protects Confidentiality and Data Security:** Microsoft Teams is used to share sensitive and confidential information that needs to be protected. When common issues such as access or permissions issues occur, it can lead to unauthorized access to confidential data. By troubleshooting these issues promptly, teams can ensure that their confidential data is secure and accessible only to authorized personnel.
- **Prevents Larger Issues:** Addressing common issues promptly can prevent them from escalating into more significant problems that can significantly affect team collaboration and productivity. For instance, if a team member is unable to access files or messages, it can lead to confusion and delay in decision-making. By troubleshooting these issues promptly, teams can prevent them from causing more significant issues that can negatively impact team performance.

Connection Issues

Microsoft Teams relies heavily on a stable and fast internet connection to function properly. When connection issues arise, it can cause significant disruptions to communication and collaboration. In this section, we will discuss the three common connection issues that users might face and how to troubleshoot them.

Slow or unstable internet connection

A slow or unstable internet connection is one of the most common connection issues that users might face while using Microsoft Teams. Symptoms of this issue include slow loading times, delayed messaging, choppy audio or video, and dropped calls.

There are several ways to troubleshoot this issue:
- **Check internet speed:** The first step in troubleshooting a slow internet connection is to check the internet speed. Users can use online tools such as Speedtest.net to measure their internet speed. If the internet speed is slow, users might consider upgrading their internet plan or contacting their internet service provider (ISP) to troubleshoot the issue.

- **Close unnecessary applications:** Running too many applications can slow down the internet connection. Users should close any unnecessary applications and browser tabs that might be using up bandwidth.
- **Use a wired connection:** Using a wired connection instead of Wi-Fi can provide a more stable and faster internet connection. If users are experiencing slow or unstable internet connection, they should try connecting their device directly to the router using an Ethernet cable.
- **Move closer to the router:** If the device is too far away from the router, the internet connection might be slow or unstable. Users should move closer to the router to improve the internet connection.
- **Disable VPN:** A virtual private network (VPN) can slow down the internet connection. Users should try disabling VPN and see if it improves the internet connection.

Firewall blocking Teams traffic

Firewalls are designed to protect the network from unauthorized access and malicious traffic. However, sometimes they can block legitimate traffic, including Microsoft Teams traffic. Symptoms of this issue include being unable to join a meeting or send messages.

There are several ways to troubleshoot this issue:

- **Check firewall settings:** The first step in troubleshooting a firewall issue is to check the firewall settings. Users should ensure that the firewall is not blocking any Teams traffic. They can also check the firewall logs for any blocked traffic.
- **Whitelist Teams traffic:** If the firewall is blocking Teams traffic, users can whitelist the Teams traffic. They can do this by adding the Teams URL or IP address to the firewall's whitelist.
- **Disable firewall;** If all else fails, users can try disabling the firewall temporarily and see if it resolves the issue. However, users should only do this as a last resort and should re-enable the firewall as soon as possible.

Outdated Teams client or browser

Using an outdated Teams client or browser can cause connection issues. Symptoms of this issue include being unable to join a meeting or send messages.

There are several ways to troubleshoot this issue:

- **Update Teams client:** The first step in troubleshooting an outdated Teams client is to update the Teams client. Users should check for any available updates and install them.
- **Clear browser cache;** If the Teams web app is not working properly, users can try clearing the browser cache. This will remove any cached data that might be causing the issue.
- **Update browser;** If the browser is outdated, users should update the browser to the latest version. Microsoft Teams supports the latest versions of Microsoft Edge, Google Chrome, Mozilla Firefox, and Apple Safari.
- **Use a different browser;** If all else fails, users can try using a different browser. They can try Microsoft Edge, Google Chrome, Mozilla Firefox, or Apple Safari to see if it resolves the issue.

Audio and video issues

Audio and video issues are some of the most common problems encountered by Microsoft Teams users. These issues can affect the quality of communication during meetings, collaboration, and general interactions in the platform. In this guide, we will discuss the most common audio and video issues that can arise in Teams and the best practices for troubleshooting them.

Microphone or camera not working

Microphone and camera issues are some of the most frustrating issues that can occur during a Teams meeting or interaction. These issues can arise due to a number of factors, including incorrect device settings, outdated drivers, and hardware malfunctions. Here are some of the most common solutions for microphone and camera issues in Teams:

- **Check device settings:** The first step in troubleshooting microphone and camera issues is to check the device settings. In Windows 10, you can access the device settings by clicking on the Start menu and searching for "Sound settings" or "Camera settings." Check to make sure that the correct microphone and camera are selected as the default devices. You should also check the device properties to ensure that the volume is not muted or set too low.
- **Update drivers:** Outdated drivers can cause microphone and camera issues in Teams. To update your device drivers, go to the device manufacturer's website and download the latest drivers for your specific device. You can also use the Device Manager in Windows 10 to update your drivers.

- **Check hardware connections:** If your microphone or camera is an external device, make sure that it is properly connected to your computer. Check the cables and ensure that the device is plugged into the correct port. If the device has a power switch or battery, make sure that it is turned on.
- **Restart Teams and the device:** Sometimes, simply restarting Teams and the device can solve microphone and camera issues. Close the Teams app, unplug any external devices, and then restart your computer. After the device has restarted, launch Teams and try to use the microphone and camera again.

Poor audio or video quality

Poor audio and video quality can be frustrating during meetings and calls. Here are some steps you can take to improve audio and video quality in Microsoft Teams:

- **Check your internet connection:** Poor audio and video quality can be caused by a slow or unstable internet connection. Try connecting to a different Wi-Fi network or using a wired connection if possible.
- **Close other apps and programs:** Running too many apps and programs at the same time can cause audio and video quality issues. Close unnecessary apps and programs before starting a Teams call or meeting.
- **Check your device settings:** Make sure that your audio and video settings are optimized for the best quality. You can adjust settings like resolution and frame rate in the Teams settings.
- **Check for app updates:** Make sure that you have the latest version of the Teams app installed. Updates often include bug fixes and improvements to audio and video features.
- **Turn off video:** If you are experiencing poor audio quality, try turning off your video during the call or meeting. This can help to reduce the amount of data being sent and improve audio quality.
- **Use a headset:** Using a headset can improve audio quality by reducing background noise and improving the clarity of your voice.

Echoes or background noise

Echoes and background noise can be distracting during calls and meetings. Here are some steps you can take to reduce or eliminate echoes and background noise in Microsoft Teams:

- **Use a headset:** Using a headset can reduce background noise and prevent echoes. Headsets with noise-canceling features are especially effective at reducing background noise.
- **Mute your microphone:** If you are not speaking, mute your microphone to prevent background noise from being picked up by other participants.
- **Use a dedicated microphone:** Using a dedicated microphone can improve audio quality and reduce background noise.
- **Change your environment:** If possible, try to have your call or meeting in a quiet environment with minimal background noise.
- **Adjust your microphone settings:** You can adjust your microphone settings in Teams to reduce background noise and echoes.

Chat and File Sharing Issues

In this section, we will discuss some of the common chat and file-sharing issues that users may encounter when using Microsoft Teams and their possible solutions.

- **Messages not sending or receiving:** One of the most common issues that users may experience when using Microsoft Teams is messages not sending or receiving. This problem can be frustrating, especially when team members need to communicate time-sensitive information. Some of the reasons why messages may not send or receive in Microsoft Teams include:
- **Internet Connectivity Issues:** Microsoft Teams relies on an internet connection to send and receive messages. If the user's internet connection is weak or unstable, it may affect the platform's ability to send and receive messages. Users can check their internet connectivity by running an internet speed test or contacting their internet service provider.
- **Outdated Teams Client:** Using an outdated version of the Teams client can also lead to messages not sending or receiving. Users should ensure that they are using the latest version of the Teams client to avoid this issue.

- **Firewall Restrictions:** Some organizations may have strict firewall restrictions that may prevent Teams from sending or receiving messages. Users can contact their IT department to verify if this is the case and ask them to whitelist Teams.
- **Server Issues:** Microsoft Teams is a cloud-based platform, which means that it relies on Microsoft's servers to send and receive messages. If Microsoft's servers are experiencing issues, it may affect the platform's ability to send and receive messages. Users can check the Microsoft Teams status page to see if there are any reported issues.
- **User Error:** Sometimes, messages may not send or receive due to user error. Users may have accidentally deleted the conversation or entered the wrong recipient's name. Users should double-check the recipient's name and ensure that they have not accidentally deleted the conversation.

Possible Solutions
- **Check Internet Connectivity:** Users should run an internet speed test to verify that their internet connection is strong and stable. They should also contact their internet service provider if they suspect that their internet connection is the issue.
- **Update Teams Client:** Users should ensure that they are using the latest version of the Teams client to avoid any issues related to outdated software.
- **Verify Firewall Restrictions:** Users should contact their I.T. department to verify if their organization has any firewall restrictions that may prevent Teams from sending and receiving messages. I.T. departments can whitelist Teams to resolve this issue.
- **Check Server Status:** Users should check the Microsoft Teams status page to see if there are any reported issues with the platform. If there are, users should wait until the issue is resolved before attempting to send or receive messages.
- **Check for User Error:** Users should double-check the recipient's name and ensure that they have not accidentally deleted the conversation. If the issue persists, users can contact Microsoft support for further assistance.

Files not uploading or downloading

One of the most common issues users face in Microsoft Teams is when files fail to upload or download. This can be a frustrating experience, especially if you're trying to share important information with your team members. There could be several reasons why this happens, and understanding the root cause can help you troubleshoot and resolve the issue.

- **Check the file size and type:** Microsoft Teams has file size and type limits, which means that you can only upload files of a certain size and type. If you're having trouble uploading a file, check its size and type to make sure it falls within the limits. For example, the maximum file size for a file uploaded to Microsoft Teams is 15 GB for SharePoint team sites and Microsoft Teams channels.
- **Check your internet connection;** Slow or unstable internet connection can cause files to fail to upload or download. Before attempting to upload or download a file, make sure your internet connection is stable and strong. You can check your internet speed using online tools like speedtest.net.
- **Check your browser:** The browser you use to access Microsoft Teams can also affect the file upload or download process. Ensure you're using a supported browser that's up to date. For the best experience, Microsoft recommends using Microsoft Edge, Google Chrome, or Mozilla Firefox.
- **Check your firewall settings:** Firewalls can also prevent files from uploading or downloading. If you have a firewall installed, make sure it's not blocking Microsoft Teams traffic. You may need to add Microsoft Teams to your firewall's exceptions list to allow it to access the internet and upload or download files.
- **Clear your cache and cookies:** Clearing your cache and cookies can also help resolve file upload or download issues. This is because cache and cookie data can accumulate over time, leading to conflicts that can affect the performance of Microsoft Teams. Clearing them can help speed up the process and improve performance.
- **Try using a different device or network:** If you're still having issues with file uploads or downloads, try using a different device or network. For example, you can switch to a different Wi-Fi network or use your mobile data network. You can also try accessing Microsoft Teams from a different device like a smartphone or tablet.

Lost or deleted messages or files

Losing important messages or files in Microsoft Teams can be frustrating, especially if you don't have a backup. However, it's possible to recover lost or deleted messages or files in Microsoft Teams. Here's what you can do:
- **Check your deleted items folder:** Microsoft Teams has a deleted items folder where deleted messages and files are temporarily stored. You can access the deleted items folder

by clicking on your profile picture and selecting 'Deleted items.' If your message or file is there, you can restore it by right-clicking on it and selecting 'Restore.'

- **Use the search feature:** If you can't find the deleted message or file in the deleted items folder, you can use the search feature to locate it. Click on the search bar at the top of the Microsoft Teams window and type in a keyword or phrase related to the message or file you're looking for. Microsoft Teams will search all your conversations and files for the keyword or phrase.
- **Check your recycle bin:** If you're unable to find the deleted message or file in the deleted items folder or through the search feature, it may have been permanently deleted. However, you can still check your recycle bin to see if it's there. You can access the recycle bin by going to SharePoint and selecting 'Recycle bin' from the left-hand side menu.
- **Contact Microsoft support:** If you're still unable to recover the lost or deleted message or file, you can contact Microsoft support for assistance. Microsoft support can help you troubleshoot the issue and find appropriate solution to the issue.

Teams meeting issues

Let's discuss some of the common Teams meetings issues, including unable to join a meeting, meeting audio or video issues, and meeting scheduling issues, and provide potential solutions to these problems.

Unable to join a meeting

One of the most frustrating issues that Teams users encounter during meetings is the inability to join a meeting. This problem can occur due to several reasons, such as incorrect meeting link or credentials, network issues, and device compatibility issues. Here are some potential solutions to this issue:

- **Check your network connection:** Ensure that your internet connection is stable and fast enough to support video conferencing. Try to disconnect and reconnect to the internet or restart your router if necessary.
- **Verify meeting link and credentials:** Double-check the meeting link or code and ensure that you are using the correct credentials to join the meeting. If you are trying to join the meeting from an external network, ensure that you have the necessary permissions to access the meeting.

- **Use the web app:** If you are having trouble joining the meeting using the Teams app, try joining the meeting through the web app using your browser. This may help you bypass some compatibility issues with the Teams app.
- **Update the Teams app:** Ensure that you are using the latest version of the Teams app. If you are using an older version, update the app to the latest version and try joining the meeting again.
- **Use another device:** If all else fails, try joining the meeting from another device, such as a tablet or smartphone. This may help you identify whether the problem is specific to your device or not.

Meeting audio or video issues

Another common issue that Teams users encounter during meetings is poor audio or video quality. This problem can be caused by several factors, such as network issues, device compatibility issues, and microphone or camera problems. Here are some potential solutions to this issue:

- **Check your network connection:** As mentioned earlier, a stable and fast internet connection is crucial for video conferencing. Try to reduce the number of devices using your network or switch to a wired connection to improve the quality of your audio and video.
- **Check device compatibility:** Ensure that your device meets the minimum requirements to use the Teams app. If you are using an external microphone or camera, ensure that it is compatible with your device and properly connected.
- **Adjust audio and video settings:** Within the Teams app, you can adjust your audio and video settings to improve the quality of your audio and video. Try to experiment with different settings, such as adjusting the volume or choosing a different microphone or camera.
- **Update the Teams app:** Ensure that you are using the latest version of the Teams app. If you are using an older version, update the app to the latest version, which may contain bug fixes and performance improvements.

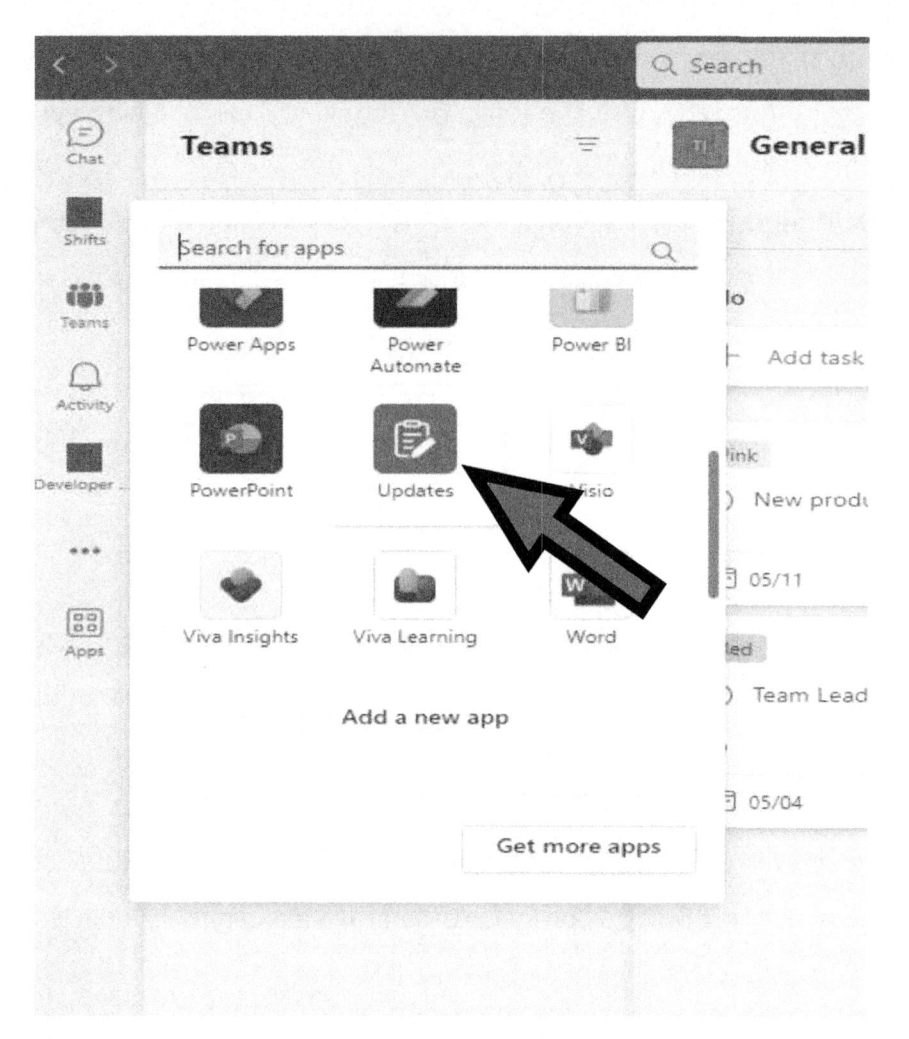

Restart the app or device: If all else fails, try restarting the Teams app or your device to see if this resolves the audio or video issues.

Meeting scheduling issues

Meeting scheduling issues can be frustrating and can cause delays or cancellations of important meetings. Microsoft Teams is an essential tool for remote communication and collaboration, and scheduling meetings is a crucial part of its functionality. However, there are some common issues that users may encounter when scheduling meetings in Teams. This guide will discuss some of the most common meeting scheduling issues in Teams and how to troubleshoot them.

Inability to Schedule Meetings

The most basic scheduling issue in Teams is the inability to schedule a meeting. This can happen due to several reasons, such as network connectivity issues, incorrect user permissions, or an outdated Teams client. To troubleshoot this issue, try the following:

- **Check your network connectivity:** Ensure that your internet connection is stable and that your device is connected to a reliable network.
- **Check your Teams client version:** Make sure that your Teams client is up-to-date. You can do this by clicking on your profile picture and selecting "Check for updates."
- **Check your user permissions:** Ensure that you have the correct permissions to schedule meetings in Teams. You can do this by going to your Teams settings and selecting "Meeting policies." Check that the settings are configured correctly.
- **Check your Teams account:** Verify that you are signed in to your Teams account. If you are signed in, sign out and then sign back in.

Scheduling Conflicts

Another common issue that users face is scheduling conflicts. This happens when a user tries to schedule a meeting during a time slot that is already occupied by another meeting. To avoid scheduling conflicts, try the following:

- **Check your availability:** Before scheduling a meeting, check your calendar to ensure that you are available at the proposed meeting time. You can do this by selecting the "Calendar" tab in Teams.
- **Use the "Scheduling Assistant" feature:** Teams offers a "Scheduling Assistant" feature that helps you find a time slot when all attendees are available. You can access this feature by clicking on the "Scheduling Assistant" tab when scheduling a meeting.
- **Reschedule conflicting meetings:** If you have already scheduled a meeting during the proposed time slot, reschedule it to avoid a scheduling conflict.

Time Zone Confusion

Time zone confusion is a common issue when scheduling meetings with participants from different time zones. This can lead to attendees showing up at the wrong time or missing the meeting altogether. To avoid time zone confusion, try the following:

- **Specify the time zone:** When scheduling a meeting, specify the time zone to avoid confusion. You can do this by selecting the "Time zone" dropdown menu and choosing the appropriate time zone.
- **Send meeting invites in the appropriate time zone:** When sending meeting invites, ensure that the meeting time is specified in the appropriate time zone.

- **Use a time zone converter:** If you are scheduling a meeting with participants from multiple time zones, use a time zone converter to determine the appropriate meeting time for each attendee.

Incorrect Meeting Details

Sometimes, users may accidentally enter incorrect meeting details when scheduling a meeting, such as the wrong time or date. This can lead to confusion and missed meetings. To avoid incorrect meeting details, try the following:

- **Double-check meeting details:** Before sending out a meeting invite, double-check the meeting details, including the date, time, and attendees.
- **Send out meeting invites early:** To allow attendees to review and confirm meeting details, send out meeting invites well in advance of the meeting.
- **Use descriptive meeting titles:** Use descriptive meeting titles that accurately reflect the meeting topic to avoid confusion.

User management Issues

User management is an essential aspect of Microsoft Teams administration. User management issues can cause significant disruptions to team collaboration, communication, and productivity. In this guide, we will discuss some common user management issues, including user access and permissions issues, user not appearing in Teams, and guest access issues.

User Access and Permissions Issues

User access and permissions issues can occur when users are unable to access certain Teams features or perform specific tasks within Teams. These issues can be caused by a variety of factors, including incorrect user permissions, Teams configuration issues, and security settings. Here are some common user access and permissions issues and their solutions:

- **User Cannot Create or Join Teams:** If a user is unable to create or join a team, it could be due to their access level. Users must have "create and join teams" permissions to create or join a team. To check user access, go to the Teams Admin Center and select Users. Locate the user and check their access level. If the user has restricted access, you can grant them "create and join teams" permissions.

- **User Cannot Access Certain Channels:** If a user cannot access certain channels within a team, it could be due to their channel permissions. By default, all members of a team can access all channels. However, team owners can restrict channel access for certain members. To check channel permissions, go to the Teams Admin Center and select Teams. Select the team in question and go to the Channels tab. Check the permissions for each channel and ensure that the user in question has the necessary permissions.
- **User Cannot Access Files or Folders:** If a user cannot access files or folders in Teams, it could be due to their file permissions. To check file permissions, go to the Teams Admin Center and select Teams. Select the team in question and go to the Files tab. Check the permissions for each file or folder and ensure that the user in question has the necessary permissions.

User Not Appearing in Teams

Sometimes, a user may not appear in Teams, despite being added to the organization. This issue can be caused by various factors, including incorrect Teams configuration, incorrect user settings, or synchronization issues. Here are some common reasons why a user may not appear in Teams and their solutions:

- **User Account Not Synced:** If a user has recently been added to the organization and is not appearing in Teams, it could be due to synchronization issues. To check the synchronization status, go to the Teams Admin Center and select Users. Locate the user and check the synchronization status. If the user's account is not synced, select the user and click the Sync button.
- **User Not Assigned a License:** If a user is not assigned a Teams license, they will not be able to access Teams. To check if a user is assigned a license, go to the Teams Admin Center and select Users. Locate the user and check if they are assigned a Teams license. If the user is not assigned a license, assign them a license.
- **User Settings Incorrect:** If a user's settings are incorrect, they may not appear in Teams. To check user settings, go to the Teams Admin Center and select Users. Locate the user and check their settings. Ensure that their Teams settings are correct.

Contacting Microsoft Teams support

There are several ways to resolve issues with Teams including, contacting Microsoft Teams support for help. Here are some of the most common options:

Microsoft Teams Help Center

The Microsoft Teams Help Center is an online resource that provides information on various topics related to Teams. It offers articles, videos, and tutorials that cover a wide range of topics, including getting started with Teams, using Teams features, troubleshooting common issues, and more. Users can browse the Help Center and find answers to their queries or search for specific topics to get more information.

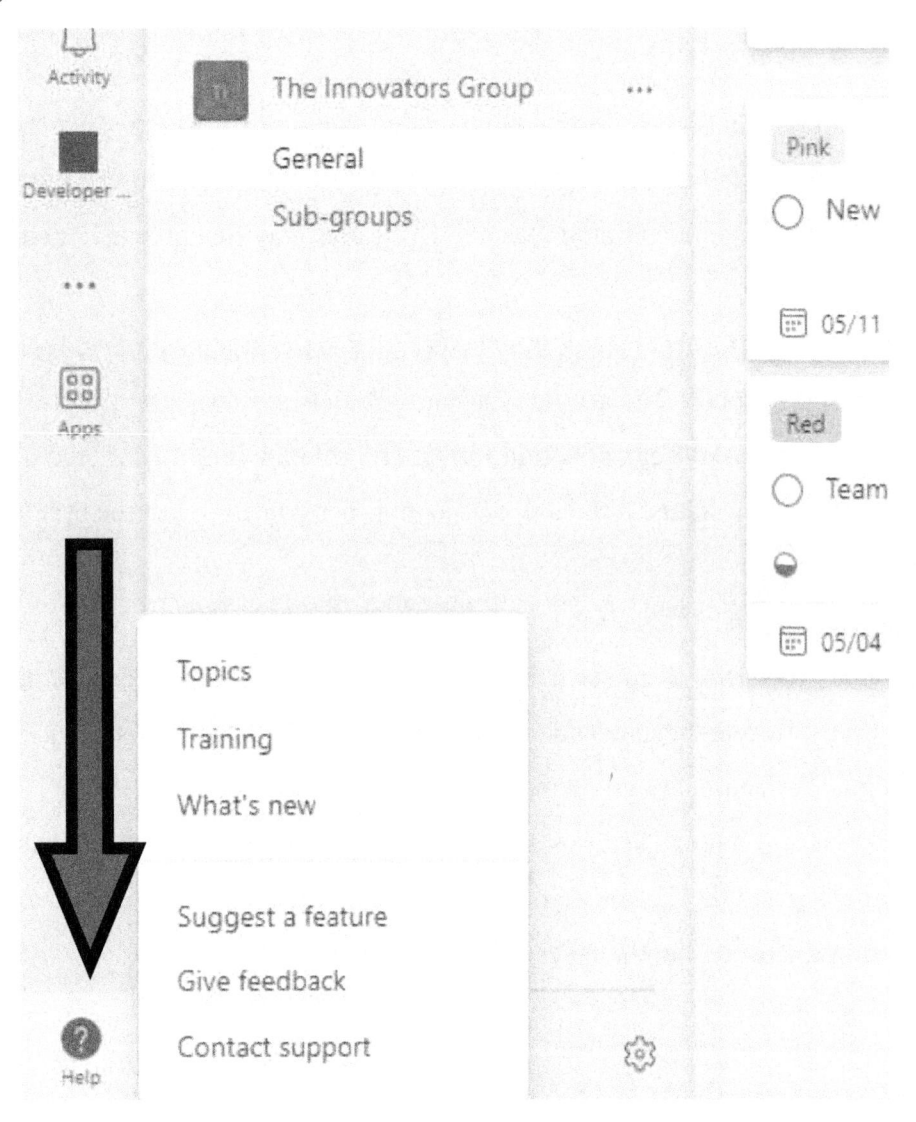

Microsoft Community

The Microsoft Community is a platform where users can ask questions and get answers from other Teams users or Microsoft experts. Users can post their queries, provide details about their issue, and receive responses from the community members. Microsoft experts also monitor the community and provide solutions to users' problems. This is a great option for users who prefer to get help from their peers.

Contacting Microsoft Support

If users cannot find a solution to their problem in the Help Center or the Community, they can contact Microsoft Support directly. Microsoft offers several options to contact support, including phone, chat, email, and social media. Users can choose the option that suits them best.

Steps to Resolve Issues with Microsoft Teams

Here are the steps involved in contacting Microsoft Teams support for help:

Step 1: Navigate to the Microsoft Teams Help Center

The first step is to navigate to the Microsoft Teams Help Center. Users can do this by typing "Microsoft Teams Help Center" in their browser's search bar or by visiting https://support.microsoft.com/en-us/teams.

Step 2: Browse or search for the desired topic

Once in the Help Center, users can browse the articles and videos or search for a specific topic using the search bar. If users are not sure what to search for, they can use the categories on the main page to find relevant articles.

Step 3: Follow the instructions in the article/video

If users find an article or video that addresses their issue, they can follow the instructions provided in the article or video to resolve the problem. Microsoft Teams Help Center provides step-by-step instructions and screenshots to make it easier for users to follow along.

Step 4: Post a question in the Microsoft Community

If users cannot find a solution in the Help Center, they can post a question in the Microsoft Community. To do this, users need to click on the "Ask the community" button on the main page of the Help Center. Users can provide details about their issue, including any error messages they received, and wait for community members to respond.

Step 5: Contact Microsoft Support

If users are unable to find a solution in the Help Center or the Community, they can contact Microsoft Support directly. To do this, users need to click on the "Contact us" button on the main page of the Help Center. Microsoft offers several options to contact support, including phone, chat, email, and social media. Users can choose the option that suits them best.

Step 6: Provide details about the issue

When contacting Microsoft Support, users need to provide details about their issue, including any error messages, steps they have already taken to resolve the problem, and any relevant information about their device or software. This will help support agents understand the problem and provide an appropriate solution.

Step 7: Follow the instructions provided by the support agent

Once users have contacted Microsoft Support, they will be connected with a support agent who will provide further assistance. The support agent may ask for additional information or request permission to remotely access the user's device to troubleshoot the issue. Users should follow the instructions provided by the support agent and provide any necessary information or access to their device.

Step 8: Follow up and provide feedback

After the issue has been resolved, users should follow up with the support agent to confirm that the problem has been resolved. Microsoft may also request feedback about the support experience, which can help improve the support process for future users.

Chapter 9

Advanced Tips and Tricks for Microsoft Teams

In this section, we'll look at some sophisticated Microsoft Teams tips and tricks, like how to use keyboard shortcuts, take advantage of time-saving tools, and adapt the app to your needs.

Keyboard Shortcuts

In Microsoft Teams, keyboard shortcuts are a great way to speed up and improve productivity. Some of the most helpful keyboard shortcuts for Microsoft Teams are listed below:

- Start a new chat with Ctrl + Shift + M.
- Ctrl + 2 to access the Calls tab
- Ctrl + 3 will take you to the Meetings tab.
- Press Ctrl + 4 to access the Files tab.
- Ctrl + 5 will take you to the Activity tab.
- Press Ctrl + 6 to access the Chat tab
- Ctrl + 7: Access the Teams tab.
- Start a new chat with the current contact by pressing Ctrl + N.
- Ctrl + E: Look for an individual or conversation
- Shift + Ctrl + X: the command window
- Shift + Ctrl + 1: Designate an important message
- Shift + Ctrl + 3: Press Ctrl + Shift + 5 to mark a message as unread: Add a picture or file to the discussion
- Shift + Ctrl + 6: beginning a video call
- Shift + Ctrl + 7: initiate a voice call
- Shift + Ctrl + B: Toggle the organizational chart open

When using Microsoft Teams, these keyboard shortcuts can help you finish tasks much faster. Consider making a custom keyboard shortcut for a feature you frequently use by using the Keyboard Shortcuts feature in Settings.

Time-saving Features

There are many tools in Microsoft Teams that can make your workday more productive. The following are some of Microsoft Teams' most practical time-saving functions:

Pinning: By pinning significant channels or chats, you can ensure that they always show up at the top of your list. Right-click on a channel or chat and choose "Pin" from the context menu.

- **Marking as read**: If you have a large number of unread messages, you can mark them all as read at once by selecting "Mark as read" from the context menu when right-clicking on a channel or chat.
- **Mute notifications**: You can turn off notifications for a particular channel or chat if you need to focus entirely on a task at hand. Right-click the channel or chat and choose "Mute notifications" to accomplish this.
- **Mentions**: Mentions are a way of letting someone know that they have been mentioned in a message. When mentioning someone, follow their name with a "@" sign.
- **Keyboard shortcuts**: As was already mentioned, using keyboard shortcuts while using Microsoft Teams can help you save a ton of time. Learn the most helpful keyboard shortcuts, and think about programming your own for features you use frequently.
- **Templates**: If you frequently produce the same kind of message or document, you might want to think about creating a template. Using a template as a starting point and then customizing it as necessary can save you time.
- **Microsoft Teams** has a robust search function that makes it easy to locate messages, files, and people. Search by typing your terms into the search bar at the top of the page.

You can quickly complete tasks using slash commands without leaving the chat window or channel you're currently in. Type "/" then the command to use a slash command.

Customizing notifications and alerts

Customizing notifications and alerts in Microsoft Teams can help you stay on top of important messages and updates without being overwhelmed by unnecessary notifications. Here are some tips for customizing notifications and alerts in Microsoft Teams:

- **Adjust notification settings**: Microsoft Teams allows you to adjust your notification settings to control which notifications you receive and how you receive them. To adjust your notification settings, click on your profile picture in the top right corner of the screen and select "Settings," then select "Notifications." Here you can choose which types of notifications you want to receive, including mentions, replies, and reactions, and how you want to receive them, such as via desktop or mobile notifications.

- **Set quiet hours**: If you don't want to be disturbed by notifications during certain times of the day, you can set "quiet hours" in Microsoft Teams. To do this, click on your profile picture in the top right corner of the screen and select "Settings," then select "Notifications." Here you can set a start and end time for your quiet hours. During quiet hours, notifications will be muted, and you won't receive any notifications on your desktop or mobile device.
- **Customize sound and vibration settings**: You can customize the sound and vibration settings for notifications in Microsoft Teams. To do this, click on your profile picture in the top right corner of the screen and select "Settings," then select "Notifications." Here you can choose the sound and vibration settings for different types of notifications, such as mentions, replies, and reactions.

- **Use focus mode**: Microsoft Teams has a focus mode feature that allows you to temporarily turn off notifications while you're working on something important. To use focus mode, click on the more options button (three dots) in the top right corner of the screen and select "Focus mode." While focus mode is on, you won't receive any notifications, and your status will be set to "Do not disturb."
- **Customize channel notifications**: You can customize the notification settings for individual channels in Microsoft Teams. To do this, click on the channel you want to customize and select the more options button (three dots) in the top right corner of the screen. Select "Channel notifications," and then choose your preferred notification settings for that channel.
- **Customize activity feed alerts**: The activity feed in Microsoft Teams shows you updates on the channels and conversations you're following. You can customize the alerts you receive in the activity feed by clicking on the more options button (three dots) in the top right corner of the screen and selecting "Manage notifications." Here you can choose which types of alerts you want to receive in your activity feed.

- **Use @mentions and priority notifications**: You can use @mentions and priority notifications to ensure that important messages get your attention. When someone mentions you in a message, you'll receive a notification. You can also set up priority notifications for specific channels or conversations. To do this, click on the channel or conversation you want to set up priority notifications for and select the more options button (three dots) in the top right corner of the screen. Select "Priority notifications," and then choose your preferred notification settings for that channel or conversation.

By customizing your notifications and alerts in Microsoft Teams, you can stay on top of important messages and updates without being overwhelmed by unnecessary notifications. Take the time to adjust your settings to meet your needs and work more efficiently with Microsoft Teams.

Creating custom bots and automations

One of the most powerful tools in Microsoft Teams is the ability to create custom bots and automations. These tools can help automate repetitive tasks, streamline workflows, and save time and effort. In this guide, we will explore how to create custom bots and automations in Microsoft Teams.

What are bots and automations?

Bots are software applications that can perform tasks automatically, without human intervention. Bots can be programmed to respond to specific keywords or phrases, and can perform a wide range of tasks, such as scheduling meetings, providing information, or sending notifications.

Automations are similar to bots, but they are typically more complex and can perform a wider range of tasks. Automations can be used to streamline workflows and automate repetitive tasks, such as creating reports, sending reminders, or updating spreadsheets.

Creating a custom bot in Microsoft Teams

Creating a custom bot in Microsoft Teams is a multi-step process that involves creating the bot, configuring its settings, and integrating it with Microsoft Teams. Here are the steps to create a custom bot in Microsoft Teams:

Step 1: Create a bot

The first step is to create a bot using a bot development platform, such as the Microsoft Bot Framework or Botpress. These platforms allow you to create bots using programming languages such as C# or JavaScript.

Step 2: Configure the bot

Once you have created the bot, you need to configure its settings. This includes defining the bot's behavior, setting up authentication, and configuring channels.

Step 3: Integrate the bot with Microsoft Teams

The final step is to integrate the bot with Microsoft Teams. This involves configuring the bot to work with Microsoft Teams and publishing the bot to the Teams app store.

Creating a custom automation in Microsoft Teams

Creating a custom automation in Microsoft Teams is a similar process to creating a bot, but it involves using a different set of tools and techniques. Here are the steps to create a custom automation in Microsoft Teams:

Step 1: Choose an automation tool

There are several automation tools that can be used with Microsoft Teams, including Power Automate (formerly known as Microsoft Flow), Zapier, and IFTTT. These tools allow you to automate workflows and tasks by creating workflows, triggers, and actions.

Step 2: Choose a trigger

The next step is to choose a trigger that will activate the automation. Triggers can include events such as receiving an email, creating a new file, or receiving a message in Microsoft Teams.

Step 3: Choose an action

Once the trigger has been set, the next step is to choose an action that will be performed automatically. Actions can include sending an email, creating a new file, or updating a spreadsheet.

Step 4: Configure the automation

The final step is to configure the automation by setting up the trigger and action, and specifying any additional settings or options.

Examples of custom bots and automations

Custom bots and automations can be used for a wide range of tasks, from scheduling meetings to updating spreadsheets. Here are some examples of custom bots and automations that can be used in Microsoft Teams:

Meeting scheduling bot: A bot that can schedule meetings automatically by checking availability and sending invites to attendees.

Expense tracking automation: An automation that can track expenses automatically by monitoring email receipts and updating a spreadsheet.

Notification bot: A bot that can send notifications automatically when specific events occur, such as a new file being uploaded or a message being received.

Knowledge base bot: A bot that can provide answers to frequently asked questions by searching a knowledge base and providing relevant information.

Onboarding automation: An automation that can streamline the onboarding process by creating user accounts, setting up permissions, and sending welcome messages.

CONCLUSION

Teams has established itself as a necessary tool for today's workplaces, allowing teams to collaborate easily whether they are based in the same location or are dispersed across the globe.

We have examined Microsoft Teams' many advantages and features in this book and demonstrated how they can support businesses in today's hectic and cutthroat marketplace. From setting up a Microsoft Teams account and adding team members to using the app to communicate, collaborate, and manage projects, everything has been covered.

The ability for teams to collaborate in real-time regardless of location is one of Microsoft Teams' major advantages. Since it enables team members to connect and collaborate effectively even when they are not in the same physical location, it is especially helpful for remote teams. Teams can work together seamlessly whether they are in the same office or on opposite sides of the world thanks to features like chat, video calls, and screen sharing.

Microsoft Teams' integrations with other Microsoft products, including Office 365, SharePoint, and OneDrive, are a significant advantage. Teams can easily share files and work together in real-time on documents thanks to these integrations without having to switch between different platforms or apps. Teams can work together on projects and documents throughout the entire process using Microsoft Teams on the same platform.

Along with a number of productivity tools, Microsoft Teams also provides calendars, automated workflows, and task management tools. By automating repetitive tasks, these features enable teams to stay organized, manage projects effectively, and free up time for more crucial work.

Tips for ongoing success with Microsoft Teams

By following the tips and best practices outlined in this book, you can unlock the full potential of Microsoft Teams and take your business to the next level.

Here are some additional tips for ongoing success with Microsoft Teams:

Stay organized: One of the key benefits of Microsoft Teams is that it allows you to keep all your team's conversations, files, and tasks in one place. However, this can also lead to information overload if you're not careful. To stay organized, create channels for different topics or projects, and use tags and filters to sort and prioritize messages and files.

Customize your notifications: Microsoft Teams can generate a lot of notifications, which can be distracting and overwhelming. To avoid this, customize your notification settings based on your preferences and work style. For example, you can choose to receive notifications only for specific channels or keywords, or turn off notifications altogether during certain times of the day.

Use keyboard shortcuts: Keyboard shortcuts can save you time and make it easier to navigate and use Microsoft Teams. Some common keyboard shortcuts include Ctrl + E to search for messages or files, Ctrl + 1 to go to your activity feed, and Ctrl + Shift + M to start a new chat.

Stay up to date with new features: Microsoft Teams is constantly evolving, with new features and updates being added on a regular basis. To stay up to date with the latest developments, join the Microsoft Teams community, attend webinars or training sessions, and follow Microsoft's official blogs and social media accounts.

Foster a culture of collaboration: Finally, to truly make the most of Microsoft Teams, it's important to foster a culture of collaboration within your team. Encourage team members to share ideas, feedback, and insights, and create a safe and supportive environment where everyone feels heard and valued. By working together and leveraging the power of Microsoft Teams, you can achieve greater success and reach your business goals faster than ever before.

Printed in Great Britain
by Amazon